AF801085

C.O.N.T.E.N.T. Solution:

7 Simple Steps for Growing Association Membership

Leona P. Dalavai Scott

© 2020 by JEP Marketing Communications LLC
PO Box 532
Bedford, Texas 76095
leona@jepmarcom.com
817.999.5899
ProfitableContentMenu.com

No part of this may be reproduced, distributed or transmitted in any form or by any means, including photocopying, recording or other electronic or mechanical methods, without the prior written permission of the publisher, except in the case of brief quotations embodied in critical reviews and certain other non-commercial uses permitted by copyright law.
ISBN No.: 978-0-578-81195-6

Dedication

For associations that are not afraid to dream big with their membership goals and aim high with their value.

For Robert, whose love and prayers make this dream of mine a reality.

Preface

One of my favorite quotes is from Arthur Ashe, *"Start where you are, use what you have, do what you can."*

Start where you are

I believe that helpful and relevant content is the secret ingredient that associations can use to get and keep members. Whether you're just starting in the field, have been serving for many years or find yourself somewhere in the middle, it's never too early – or late – to do a better job of serving your membership with content that solves their problems to deliver membership value.

Use what you have

Creating content that consistently delivers value is not easy. That's why this workbook includes a seven-part C.O.N.T.E.N.T. framework to guide you in making it easier. The framework is a culmination of my many years of experience creating content for associations – first as a communications coordinator, later as an editor and most recently overseeing marketing and communications teams. By sharing the framework, I hope you will avoid some of the mistakes I made to guide you to greater and faster success.

As a bonus, I've included a content planning calendar to give you a step-by-step action plan to keep you on track of creating content, while also reaching your membership goals. This workbook should be an interdepartmental effort – led by the team(s) that are responsible for creating content – while getting regular input from the membership department and/or sales teams, along with other association leadership for regular accountability to ensure you stay on track to meet your membership goals.

Do what you can

The goal of this workbook is to be your guide and accountability on the path to creating content that delivers value while helping you get and keep members. Use it, refer to it, dog ear it and come back to it often to keep yourself accountable. I have to do this almost daily. Even after creating regular content for more than 20 years, the process can be just as daunting for me. But having the 7-part framework – and a written plan for content creation – keeps me on track to accomplish my goals.

So I encourage you to stay focused, be consistent and keep your member's needs and problems top of mind, and you will succeed. It takes time, commitment, consistency and a content plan to accomplish your membership goals. It's my hope that this workbook will guide you along that path with greater clarity and details so that your association will continue to serve your members with valuable content for the next 100 years.

Contents

Introduction: I See You 6

Chapter 1 Clarify your ideal audience 9

Chapter 2 Organize your content sources or "plates" into a calendar 13

Chapter 3 Narrate your story to address a problem 17

Chapter 4 Tailor your content to a customer's journey 21

Chapter 5 Establish your value by providing a solution 23

Chapter 6 Nourish your audience consistently 27

Chapter 7 Test, analyze, and recalibrate 31

Planner Section Content Creation Plan and Implementation Process 37

Accountability Scoreboard Templates 59

Quarter 1 60

Quarter 2 78

Quarter 3 96

Quarter 4 114

Yearly Membership Scoreboard 132

About the Author 134

Introduction: I See You

You're an association executive with a lot on your plate. You're juggling an ever-growing list of responsibilities, expectations and revenue goals. You know have a lot to offer, and you know your association has done a lot of good in your industry. But your membership numbers are still trending down. In fact, it's been that way for a while but you're at a loss on what to do. You've tried many different solutions, but none of them work. And time is running out.

So you continue doing what you do best – creating content that you hope will provide value for your members. You see your Membership Department struggling to meet their goals, falling behind month after month, year after year. Working together, you come up with a membership marketing plan with input from your Board, your executive leadership team, and others at the helm of your organization. You get off to a strong start, but like a bad car crash, you're broadsided with several challenges, leaving your association on critical life support.

Those challenges result in some negative press and tarnish your reputation in the industry. There are pointing fingers, leadership struggles, and high staff turnover. Once again, you fail to meet your membership goals.

You're frustrated and wondering if you're ever going to see your association grow again. You wonder if you should just quit and start looking for another job.

But deep down, your inner voice is urging you not to quit. You know your association can serve more people and change their lives, careers, and businesses for the better. You know because you've seen it. But how do you get there? How do you turn things around with even fewer resources than before?

Do you dream of having more members?

Is your retention rate not what it used to be (like in the "good old days")?

Do you dread publishing your annual report with the membership growth chart arrow trending downward?

Do you fear facing your board and losing your job if you don't increase membership?

Do you feel responsible for laying off staff as a result of declining membership revenue?

Do you wonder how to deliver five-star service and relevant benefits when you have a smaller staff?

Are you staying up at night worrying about how you're going to "fix it" without any new ideas or solutions?

Do you find yourself working more weekends than ever, causing your spouse to worry about your stress level and health?

It doesn't have to be this way.

Imagine turning your dream of more members into reality.

Instead of staying up at night, you can sleep better knowing that you have a plan to increase membership and retention.

You will be a stronger, more confident leader for your association because you will be taking clear action to turn your membership around and tie your content into your membership goals.

Instead of being stressed, you can clear your mind of worries. You can create relevant and helpful content that helps lead your association to the kind of growth it hasn't seen in a long time. Not to mention, you will win the approval of your board with the results and progress you've made.

Instead of working weekends, you will have a greater work-life balance that will allow you to enjoy time with your family and enjoy your hobbies.

Ready to get started?

Know Your Gap to Get Your Map

I remember one of my favorite family vacations as a kid. We traveled from Kansas to Texas one summer to enjoy Six Flags Over Texas and a Rangers ballgame.

It was an eight-hour road trip, and my dad had no idea how to get there. Like other fathers of his generation, he relied on a Rand McNally Road Atlas. (Remember those?)

Just like my dad relied on his atlas to get us to Texas, you have a destination in mind when it comes to your membership goals. How do you get from A to Z? And what needs to happen in between to reach your destination? Yogi Berra said, "If you don't know where you are going, you'll end up someplace else." Don't end up someplace else.

To get your juices flowing, answer three simple questions:

> How many members does your association currently have?
> This is called your **departure** number. _________
>
> How many members does your association want to have in the next 12 months? This is your **destination** number. _________
>
> What is your **gap**? Subtract your departure number from your destination number. _________

You will transfer your answers onto the chart on the following page.

Here is an example:

ABC Association currently has 4500 members. It wants to have 4700 members in the next 12 months. The gap between their destination and departure is 200 (4700 – 4500).

Here is ABC's summary:

Measurements	Departure	Gap	Destination
Members	4500	200	4700

Now use the template below to write your answers from page 7:

Measurements	Departure	Gap	Destination
Members			

Closing the Gap

Once you've identified your gap, you'll be ready to take action to close it. But what action should you take? I believe this workbook is your answer – atlas, if you will.

This workbook will help you create the content you need using my unique C.O.N.T.E.N.T creation framework. In the planning section, I will help you map out the plan and implement it so you can close the gap and reach your membership destination.

For membership organizations, content can be a cost-effective way to get and keep members. Associations are leaders when it comes to creating content – from annual meetings to publications to videos and everything in between.

Let's first define what "content" is. The Content Marketing Institute defines content as "Compelling information that informs, engages, or amuses." Good content can help grow and strengthen association membership, which has been on the decline since 1994. If used strategically, content can help bridge many gaps when it comes to membership growth and retention.

And most important, good content can deliver member value in a way that taps into all of your association departments for an orchestrated and successful effort in getting and keeping members.

Chapter 1

Clarify your ideal audience

> STEP 1: The first step in our C.O.N.T.E.N.T. system is the letter "C."

Objective: Clarify your ideal audience.

To have effective content, you must clarify your ideal member/customer. I use these terms interchangeably because members are our customers, right? Please *do not* skip this step – be crystal clear on who you're serving as a membership organization! Jumping right in to creating content may seem easy, but you first need to clarify who that content is for.

So often, associations make the mistake of "knowing" their members and assuming that they like certain topics or content. The member you knew last year may not be the same member you're serving today. When was the last you had a conversation with a member? Or better yet, visited a member in their workplace? If you haven't spent some time lately getting to know your members, do it now. And don't underestimate the importance of a good old phone call. In this new digital age, people are looking for greater connections than a text or email. Hearing and talking to a human voice is powerful, and when in-person visits can't happen, a phone call can be a helpful substitute.

I promise – the time you spend getting to know your members will be worth the investment. As a result, your content will be more effective, engaging, compelling, and relevant. Pretty soon, your members and prospects will be thinking, *How can they read my mind so well?* Those regular touchpoints will help you connect with members in a real and authentic way that will be reflected in your content.

Clarifying your audience will help you understand who you're writing for. Often, an association will have several audience segments. If you are able to write to multiple audiences, do it. If not, start with your most important audience segment, and you can develop content for additional segments later. We'll be addressing audience segments in more detail in Step 4 – Tailor Your Content to a Customer's Journey.

Let's look at an example of how to clarify your audience.

WHAT

What is the problem? Let's say an association is struggling to get new members and retain their existing membership. It's been a while since they've done a membership survey or interviewed members to find out their needs and what they are struggling with. They have a list of problems that they address, but their membership is changing and those problems may or may not still be relevant. Baby boomers, who make up a bulk of their membership, are retiring, and younger members are either slow to join or don't see a lot of value in the current package.

WHY

Why is it important to clarify your audience? If you don't know who your audience is and what their common challenges, pain points, or struggles are, how are you going to help them solve a problem? By clarifying your audience, you are able to go after customers with specific problems. Don't waste your time, money, or energy chasing after the wrong customers who either don't need your membership offerings or don't realize the value and wouldn't pay for your membership.

HOW

How do you clarify your audience? Talk to your existing ideal customers. According to online marketing expert Amy Porterfield, your ideal customers—commonly referred to as your "ideal customer avatar" (ICA for short)—are people who want and need your content, product, or service. These are also people whom you LOVE to work with. So it's a win-win for your association and your members.

Getting to know your ideal members doesn't have to be overwhelming. There are so many tools and resources at our fingertips to make the process simple and efficient. Here are some ways to get to know your ideal members:

- **Use your Facebook Group or online communities:** Spend some quality time reading through the topics to see what issues, problems, or pain points come up. Consider including regular polls or post a question to your group about problems they're experiencing. Start the conversation and *listen* to what they have to share.
- **Use surveys:** Short ones work best. Or consider doing several short surveys with just a few questions so as not to overwhelm your audience. Share the surveys in your Facebook Group or in your online communities to get regular feedback.
- **Ask them** during phone interviews, in-person conversations, or videoconferences.
- **Send them an email.**
- **Interview them at events or virtual gatherings:** Have a list of prepared questions handy to be respectful of their time. For virtual gatherings, don't forget to download the Chat discussions. Chats are similar to the comments section of your social media conversations. They are a treasure trove of great questions and problems that are on the minds of your members and ICA.
- **Text them** if you have that comfort level with your members.

What should you ask members?

As you talk to ideal members, here are some helpful topics to start the conversation. The point in asking these questions is to get a well rounded picture of who your ideal members are. Remember, the goal here is to clarify your audience. You can ask questions like:

- What are your biggest challenges, struggles, or pain points related to your business and career? Tie those pain points into how you will serve them as an association.
- What does a typical day look like for you?
- What do you like to do in your free time? What are your hobbies, what shows do you watch, who do you follow online? What is your favorite social media platform?
- What does your family life look like? Are you single or married? Do you have kids at home, and what are their ages?
- What's your highest education level? What are your personal or career goals? What are their dreams – both professionally and personally?
- Which magazines do you read? Do you listen to podcasts or read books?

HERE IS AN EXAMPLE of an association that wanted to clarify its audience to create better value. The International Casual Furnishings Association (ICFA) wanted to increase engagement and participation from its Millennial and Gen Z audiences. So it used its annual educational conference to highlight young members' voices and get them involved in its annual conference.

As a result of ICFA's efforts, Millennial and Gen Z content leaders presented on relevant topics to a multigenerational audience. The conference not only boosted young-member engagement, it also engaged its entire membership base – from retailers, manufacturers, and suppliers to service providers and designers. By reaching out to the younger generations, ICFA got them involved and active, which is key to membership retention.

Now, it's your turn.

What is a specific problem that you are trying to solve as an association? List some problem(s) you're trying to solve. You may find that you have more than one problem you're trying to address. Remember: one specific measurable problem to one specific audience. You may also find that your association has more than one audience segment (for example, baby boomers, Gen Z, or millennials). Select a specific problem for a specific audience. The more you talk to your members and audience, the more educated and knowledgeable you will feel.

As you address a problem for your audience, ask yourself about the symptoms that make up the problem. For example, the ICFA had the problem of lack of involvement and interest in their association by younger generations. The symptom of that problem was low attendance at its conference. The solution is the ICFA gets their younger members involved in planning and developing the content for the conference so they are more likely to attend and be engaged.

MEMBER (AUDIENCE) SEGMENT	MEMBER (AUDIENCE) PROBLEM
1)	
2)	
3)	
4)	
5)	
6)	
7)	
8)	
9)	
10)	

Chapter 2

Organize your content sources or "plates" into a calendar

> The second step in our C.O.N.T.E.N.T. system is the letter "O."

Objective: Organize your content sources or "plates" into a content calendar.

As content creators, we are often juggling multiple "plates," so I often refer to content sources as "plates."

Make a list of all of your content plates (magazine, podcast, social media, email marketing, workshop, annual conference, blog, etc.) and also the platforms on which you publish your content. Seeing a complete list of your content sources and platforms will make gathering content easier. Organize your content plates based on how often your audience is consuming them, or in order of priority. For example, if you post to your social media accounts Monday through Friday, you would list social media and add the frequency as five times per week.

WHAT

What is the problem? Often, there are so many spinning plates for an association, and you may not have taken the time to organize them in an effective manner. By not staying organized or developing a content calendar, you may drop one of those spinning plates and fail to deliver timely and relevant content that provides value for your audience. The more value you provide, the more you will connect and engage with your audience, which helps you get and keep members.

WHY

Why is it important to organize your content plates? Organizing your content by plates and publication schedule makes setting up your content calendar easier and more effective because you're planning your content, deadlines, and production schedule in advance. Since a membership cycle is most often based on a year-round calendar, it makes sense to establish your content calendar on a year-round basis.

HOW

How do you organize your content plates? Spend a few minutes listing all of your content plates. Here's a quick list of some common content plates of associations to get you started:

- Social media
- Email
- Newsletter
- Direct mail
- Magazine
- Podcast
- Webinar
- Annual meeting
- Workshops
- Forums

LET'S LOOK AT AN EXAMPLE of an association that is adapting its content plates to different generations. The American Association of Retired Persons (AARP) introduced a project in 2017 called The Girlfriend, which aims to reach Gen X women in their mid 40s to early 50s to start building conversations with their soon-to-be members. It introduced a variety of streaming videos and an e-newsletter.

Existing AARP readers, comprising mainly of baby boomers, had a popular monthly print magazine. But wanting to "prime the pump" for these future members, AARP introduced new content in formats that appealed to this particular audience. These 40-something women are also active on Facebook, and

The Girlfriend has built a strong following on that platform as well. Remember: your audience type, including generation, can often dictate your content plate.

Now it's your turn.

What are all of your association's content plates, and with what frequency do you use them? I've listed a few to get you started.

CONTENT PLATE	FREQUENCY
SOCIAL MEDIA	
NEWSLETTER	
DIRECT MAIL	
WEBINAR	
ANNUAL MEETING	

Notes

Chapter 3

Narrate your story to address a problem

> The third step in our C.O.N.T.E.N.T. system is the letter "N."

Objective: Narrate your story to address a problem.

Now comes the fun part: putting your content together in the form of a story. *In What's Your Story,* author Craig Wortmann says stories are effective because they cut through the noise, giving people something they can bite into and build stronger connections with.

From Step 1, you have a list of your members' problems. Now, narrate their problems with a story, showing empathy and care. By sharing in their journey and practicing empathy, you are caring for your customers and building the foundation for a long-lasting, trusting relationship. Zig Ziglar said, "People will *listen* to you if they like you. But they will do business with you if they trust you."

WHAT

What do you need to narrate a story? As you'll recall from English class, a good story has a beginning, a crisis, and a *resolution.*

WHY

Why should you narrate your story? Stories are powerful. They show instead of just tell. Human beings are made for stories, and storytelling is a powerful tool to persuade your audience on the value of what your association has to offer. A story can capture your audience's interest in a way that makes them want to belong to your association.

HOW

How do you narrate your story? If you've spent time clarifying your audience in Step 1, you should have a good idea of who your ideal members (or characters in your story) are. Paint a picture of who your members are, what challenges they face, and how your association helps them solve those challenges.

HERE'S AN EXAMPLE of how you can use story to paint a picture.

At the beginning of the story, **introduce your character who is facing a problem.**

In our example, a long-time association executive director in her late 50s must turn around membership within a year, or she will be replaced by someone who can. She is at the end of her rope, having tried many things without results.

The crisis is that membership is declining. To address the problem, she holds a two-day board and staff retreat to brainstorm and come up with ideas and solutions. Aided by research from a recent association study, the group outlines ways to get younger generations to join their association. They identify four key areas of interest:

- Leadership opportunities
- Mentoring
- Year-round training access
- Making a difference

The resolution is that the association adds new benefits and opportunities that address these primary areas. For example, they decide to introduce a new mentoring program that matches younger members with experienced members who can offer the kind of direction, wisdom, and insights these younger members crave. They also create short-term leadership opportunities through specialized committees that allow younger members to serve but don't involve a long-term commitment. They also create a new certification program that addresses their need to build their skillset to gain job security. The two-day retreat—while exhausting—is successful. All of the parties leave with a specific, actionable plan to implement with regular accountability meetings to ensure they stay on track.

As a result of implementing these ideas, the association sees its membership grow by five percent within the first 15 months. This growth gives them the results and affirmation they need to know that they are on the right track.

Now, it's your turn.

Look at your ideal members. What problems have they experienced that your association can help them with?

Beginning: Paint a picture of a member with a problem. How do they feel? What are they thinking?

Crisis: Identify their problem.

Resolution: Show how your association helped them to solve that problem. This is the transformation part of your story. At the beginning, you showed how the member was before they received help from your association. Now show the "after" transformation, where they've solved a key problem that they faced.

For more information on the topic of storytelling, read *Building a StoryBrand: Clarify Your Message So Your Customers Will Listen* by Donald A. Miller.

BEGINNING OF STORY	
CRISIS (PROBLEM)	
RESOLUTION (HOW PROBLEM WAS SOLVED)	

Notes

Chapter 4

Tailor your content to a customer's journey

> The fourth step in our C.O.N.T.E.N.T. system is the letter "T."

Objective: Tailor your content to a customer's journey.

As you write down problems your customers face, see if there are certain categories that come up repeatedly – for example, finance, customer service, or marketing. You want to develop content that addresses the specific needs of your audience.

WHAT

What types of content do you tailor to your audience? It depends on what their needs are. The more you talk with your ideal members in step 1, the more you'll see certain topics coming up over and over again.

WHY

Why should you tailor your content? Tailoring your content to the different needs of your audience creates better value for your association members. Members are more likely to get value from topics that resonate with them and address their needs.

HOW

How should you tailor your content? You can tailor content by different issues, or even by different segments of your audience and membership types.

FOR EXAMPLE, ASAE, the Center for Association Leadership (ASAE), serves the needs of all association professionals. It tailors its content by the specific departments found in associations, including Administrative, Membership, Marketing & Communications, Legislative Advocacy, and Events. They then rotate content for these specific segments of the organization. They also structure their magazine, newsletter and online communities, for example, by the various interests of specific departmental members.

Now, it's your turn.

Write down the different types of member segments your association has. Categorize it by topic or interest area.

MEMBER SEGMENT/TYPE	TOPIC/INTEREST AREA

Chapter 5

Establish your value by providing a solution

> The fifth step in our C.O.N.T.E.N.T. system is the letter "E."

Objective: Establish your value by providing a solution.

Give your audience solutions to their problems. By positioning your association as the solution provider, you are helping them solve the problem they're facing.

WHAT

What types of solutions should you offer? Once again, this goes back to clarifying your audience (see why step 1 is so important?). The better you know your audience, the better you'll understand what their everyday problems are so you can tailor your content accordingly. Ideal members' problems change daily, so check in regularly to ensure you're delivering content with relevant solutions.

WHY

Why should you offer different solutions? People are not one-dimensional. Consider the various problems you face in a single day. In the morning, you might be dealing with that squeaky noise as you drive your car. At night, you're deciding what to feed your picky toddler for dinner. All day long, you're wondering how you're going to finish that work project when you don't have everything you need to get it done. Your members are the same way. Offer a variety of content to appeal to the range of problems they experience.

HOW

How should you offer these solutions? There are so many different ways to deliver solutions through your content. Consider social media, videos, email newsletters, magazines, podcasts, workshops, etc. Look at all of your different content plates to assess your opportunities.

FOR EXAMPLE, Pink Petro is a 11,000-member, Houston-based company transforming the association landscape with innovative and relevant solutions for women in the oil and gas, power and utilities and renewables industries. Since its founding in 2014, Pink Petro had addressed problems facing the energy industry, including a poor public image, an aging demographic, and gender diversity. Pink Petro structures all of its content to address these problems.

Each month, Pink Petro offers a members-only Coach's Corner, taught by an instructor or trainer who gives private or specialized teaching. Leaders from the energy community worldwide join the CEO host and founder for a conversation and Q & A on a variety of topics that are applicable to association members. The Coach's Corner webinar provides solutions to the leading questions and problems their members are facing.

Now, it's your turn.

How are you addressing your member's biggest problems, and what plates are you using to address them?

PROBLEM	SOLUTION	CONTENT PLATE

Notes

Chapter 6

Nourish your audience consistently

> The sixth step in our C.O.N.T.E.N.T. system is the letter "N."

Objective: Nourish your audience consistently.

This is a biggie that many associations overlook. You must have a plan to share your content. Planning ahead makes your content calendar implementable. If you don't plan ahead, consistency is difficult, as is delivering relevant content.

One of the key benefits to developing a content calendar is helping association staff collaborate with other departments on a variety of engagement opportunities. With the right calendar and processes in place, you can schedule content, marketing, emails, and social media campaigns to coincide weeks, months, or even a year in advance.

Make sure you are touching your ideal members on a daily, weekly, monthly, quarterly, and annual basis to mirror the membership cycle. Creating value year-round makes the "should I renew?" question much easier to answer.

WHAT

What type of content should be used and when? Look at your workbook exercise in step 2, where you listed your content plates and frequency.

WHY

Why should you plan specific content for specific times of the year? To make your content work as effectively as possible, you need to be consistent and strategic. For example, a new member who has joined recently may have different content needs than a long-time member. They may be more interested in content that orients them to your association, how they can get involved, and your value proposition. Introducing a new benefit or launching something new? Quarterly webinars or workshops are great for delivering new information or training and education. And of course, your association's annual conference is an ideal opportunity to deliver valuable content to members who are new or celebrating many years of membership.

HOW

How should you plan your content? Using your exercises from step 2 and step 4 (now is a good time to review), plan your content based on the daily, weekly, monthly, quarterly, and annual frequency timeline. Look at what your association's goals and activities are, and schedule your content accordingly.

FOR EXAMPLE, the University of Kansas' Alumni Association structures its content calendars for various communication channels throughout the year. Its marketing team organizes campaigns around five seasons in a 12-month time period. In February, it shows its membership love by promoting the Member APPreciation Month – where its promotions are centered around an exclusive, members-only benefit available through its mobile app to encourage downloads and engagement. Beginning in March, after basketball season, it includes membership promotions. In May, after graduation, it begins promoting memberships to recent graduates. In the fall, it promotes memberships to returning alumni who don't already belong. In November-December, it has holiday pushes for gift memberships and year-end gifts over and above membership dues (especially for Life Members who paid their dues years ago). Review your association's annual year-round schedule to plan your content around specific initiatives and events.

Now, it's your turn.

How can you structure your association content to nourish your audiences year-round?

MEMBER SEGMENT/TYPE	PROBLEM/ ISSUE/FOCUS/GOAL	CONTENT PLATE	FREQUENCY

Notes

Chapter 7

Test, analyze, and recalibrate

> The seventh and final step in our C.O.N.T.E.N.T. system is the letter "T."

Objective: Test, analyze, and recalibrate.

When you're sharing content and valuable solutions with your audience, you need to see what is resonating and connecting with them. Regularly review your engagement, feedback, data, and analytics to see what is working and not. **Remember, the only message that resonates is the one that helps the member solve a problem.**

WHAT

What should you be testing? On your social media platforms, you can use a channel's built-in analytics tools. Same goes for your email marketing campaigns—check your email service provider's dashboard. For your website and blog, look at your google analytics to see which pages and resources people are accessing. And for events, you can use attendee surveys to solicit feedback.

WHY

Why should you be testing? If you never test or measure anything, how do you know that your content is delivering value to your members? It's the classic "throwing spaghetti at the wall and seeing what sticks" scenario. Quit doing that; it doesn't work.

Keep in mind that some content falling flat doesn't mean it's not resonating. In a busy, distraction-filed age, people need to see something six to eight times or even more before they take action. Promote your content across your different content plates such as social media, newsletter, blog, podcast, etc. Consider also that a different headline, new copy, or even a new graphic might perform better.

HOW

How should you be testing? Schedule regular analytics and engagement reviews right into your calendar. The ASAE Foundation's 2019 study, Association Content Strategies for a Changing World, found that measuring data is impossible without established metrics. Knowing your baselines allows your staff to

- analyze whether content is valuable or successful;
- make data-driven decisions about new content; and
- improve existing content, set goals for beating current baselines, and provide even greater member value.

Depending on your systems, database, and dashboard platforms, the level of sophistication and what you can measure can vary greatly.

FOR EXAMPLE, the American Association of Airport Executives merged its database with its content-management system and email marketing platform for a powerful, data-driven experience. To help with registrations to its annual conference, AAAE began tracking engagement on its conference landing page. It set parameters to flag visitors who clicked on five or more links. Based on their engagement, the association delivered an automated email campaign of four emails over a 20-day period to educate them about the conference's value, benefits, and key learning objectives. One of its messages was a justification letter that prospective attendees could present to their employer. As a result, the association saw a 25% boost in registrations from the previous year, resulting in an additional $15,000 in revenue.

Members-only content is another opportunity to measure member engagement.

Review the analytics in your association management system to see which pages and content are resonating. Many AMS platforms can personalize content with articles, ads, and product links based on individual member interests. This frees up staff time to work on other content or focus directly on one-on-one member interactions.

Now, it's your turn.

List some specific measurables that you can track through your content to help improve member value.

Content	What You're Measuring

Notes

Conclusion

While the story I'm about to tell is fictional, you may recognize that some of details may apply to your association. Once upon a time, there was an association called The American Association. The 60-year-old organization is based in Oak Park, Illinois, just outside of Chicago. It has 6,500 members and twenty-two full-time staff members. For the last five years, it has seen a steady decline in membership. Many of their existing members are baby boomers, and as they were retiring, they weren't renewing.

Unfortunately, the association didn't have a robust strategic plan in place to recruit younger members into their association. As a result, they saw a steady decline in membership (see the domino effect taking place)? And due to declining membership dues, they didn't have the resources or funding to introduce new programs or benefits.

To address the declining member revenue, the association had to lay off several key staff members and weren't able to deliver some of their membership services and benefits as effectively as before.

For example, they had to cut their magazine from monthly to quarterly distribution. They had to eliminate their popular, highly engaging workshops in regional events throughout the country because they drained travel budgets and over extended its staff's capabilities.

It was a shame, because their members loved these events. They got to attend some relevant training and hear some inspirational speakers. Its members always went back to their businesses refreshed and full of great ideas with a clear action plan for implementation. Plus, if they had questions about their membership or wanted to renew, the always-helpful AA staff was there to take care of them, providing concierge-level of service and attention.

As a result of declining revenue, the association decided to raise dues ... and how do you think members responded – by renewing?

No. They canceled their memberships.

Now, the above is a fictional story, but it's rooted in truth. This scenario is happening more often than you may think. And we may be seeing more scenarios like this as a result of these new normal times and the financial impact on members. That is troubling, because associations have a huge role to play in our careers, personal lives, and society in general.

John Graham, the former president of the American Society of Association Executives, who passed away in January 2020, had this to say on the value of associations:

"Associations can also continue to advocate for solutions to our nation's problems. Associations amplify the voice of the industries and people they represent, and they lend expertise and real-world experience to policymakers who choose to listen and who want to achieve results for their constituencies.

"Associations have a huge responsibility to the world. We understand that our stakeholders extend beyond just the members and volunteers we represent, to the communities in which we live and work and the far regions of the world where some innovation or standard we perpetuate helps improve someone's quality of life."

All association content creators – whether from the membership department, marketing and communications, or events – want to deliver value. Think about it: without good content, association members would starve and become deficient in all areas of their lives. But content that feeds and nourishes your members will keep them healthy, strong and coming back year after year for a lifetime.

Here is a summary of the seven-step CONTENT creation process

CLARIFY: Content is clear on its intended audience

ORGANIZED: Content is organized by content plate into a calendar

NARRATE YOUR STORY: Content is entertaining and includes story, if possible

TAILORED TO AUDIENCE: Content reflects the member's journey

ESTABLISH VALUE: Content is relevant and has helpful solutions

NOURISH: Audience receives consistent content

TEST: Content is reviewed and analyzed regularly to promote better engagement for future

Now that we have completed your content creation framework, it is time to develop your planning and implementation process so you can reach your membership goals.

PLANNER SECTION

Content Creation Plan and
Implementation Process

There are four major steps in this planning and implementation process
Here is an overview:

1. Develop your map
2. Design Your Content Blueprints
3. Design Your Content Creation Calendar
4. Develop Accountability Scoreboards

Let's dive into each of the four major steps in greater detail:

Major Step 1: Develop Your Map

To develop an accurate map for your organization, take the follow mapping steps (as you may recall, this is what we did in Know Your Gap to Get Your Map section on page 7.)

1. Determine your departure numbers
2. Determine your destination numbers and gap
3. Develop your map

An accurate map is developed using two profitable membership rate templates. The two profitable membership rates are:

1. Conversion Rate – getting new members
2. Retention Rate – keeping existing members

Let's follow Steps 1-3 to develop a map for ABC Association:

Mapping Step 1: Determine Your Departure Numbers

Last year, the ABC Association had 5000 members. During the year, it generated 2000 membership leads and were able to convert 200 of them into new members. ABC ended the year with 4500 members. In the next 12 months, ABC Association wants to increase their membership from 4500 to 5000.

Let's answer some questions based on ABC's numbers to make sure you understand the mapping process.

✔ ***Question:*** How many leads did ABC generate last year?
✔ ***Answer:* 2000**

✔ ***Question:*** How many new members did ABC add to their membership?
✔ ***Answer:* 200**

✔ ***Question:*** What was ABC's conversion rate last year?
✔ ***Answer:* 10%**

- ✔ ***Question:*** How many leads does ABC currently have in their funnel? To simplify the development of the map, let's just say 0.
- ✔ ***Answer:*** 0

How did we arrive at the conversion rate of 10%? We simply divided the number of new members (200) by the number of leads generated (2000). So, 200 ÷ 2000 = 10%

- ✔ ***Question:*** What was ABC's retention rate last year?
- ✔ ***Answer:*** 86%

How did we arrive at the retention rate of 86%? We simply divided the retained number: 4500 – 200 = (4300) by the membership number at the beginning of the year (5000). So, 4300 ÷ 5000 = 86%.

Let us see what ABC's Conversion and Retention departure column looks like:

Conversion Rate Template			
Conversion Measurements	**Departure**	**Gap**	**Destination**
Leads	0		
Conversion Rate	10%		
New Members	0		

Retention Rate Template			
Retention Measurements	Departure	Gap	Destination
Members	4500		
Retention Rate	86%		

Now, it's your turn to answer some questions to determine your departure numbers. You will transfer your answers onto the charts on the following page.

- ✔ ***Question:*** How many leads did your organization generate last year? If you don't know or don't have any record, your answer should be zero.
- ✔ ***Answer:*** ___________

- ✔ ***Question:*** How many new members did you add to your association or business?
- ✔ ***Answer:*** ___________

- ✔ ***Question:*** What was your conversion rate? Simply divide the number of new members by the number of leads generated last year as in the example above.

- ✔ ***Answer:*** ___________ **% Enter your answer in the conversion rate row under the departure column.**

- ✔ ***Question:*** How many leads does your association or business currently have in your funnel? Again, if you don't know or don't have any record, simply put in zero. By using zero, this will simplify your map.
- ✔ ***Answer:*** __________ **Enter your answer in the leads row under the departure column.**

- ✔ ***Question:*** How many members did your association or business have at the beginning of the year?
- ✔ ***Answer:*** __________

- ✔ ***Question:*** How many members did your association or business have at the end of the year?
- ✔ ***Answer:*** __________ **Enter your answer in the members row under the departure column in your retention rate template below.**

- ✔ ***Question:*** What was your retention rate last year? Simply divide the retained number: (End of year number minus new members) by the membership number at the beginning of the year as in the example above.
- ✔ ***Answer:*** __________ % **Enter your answer in the retention rate row under the departure column in your retention rate template below:**

Conversion Rate Template			
Conversion Measurements	**Departure**	**Gap**	**Destination**
Leads			
Conversion Rate			
New Members			

Retention Rate Template			
Retention Measurements	Departure	Gap	Destination
Members			
Retention Rate			

Mapping Step 2: Determine Your Destination Numbers and Gap

To determine your destination and calculate your gap, you need to answer more questions following ABC Association's example.

- ✔ ***Question:*** How many members does ABC Association want to have in the next 12 months?
- ✔ ***Answer:*** **4700 Members**

- ✔ ***Question:*** *What is ABC Association's desired retention rate in the next 12 months?*
- ✔ ***Answer:*** **90%**

- ✔ ***Question:*** How many new members does ABC Association need to have in the next 12 months?
- ✔ ***Answer:*** **650 New Members (4700 – 90%*4500)**

- ✔ ***Question:*** *What is the ABC Association's desired conversion rate in the next 12 months?*
- ✔ ***Answer:*** **20%**

- ✔ ***Question:*** *How many leads does ABC Association need in the next 12 months?*
- ✔ ***Answer:*** **3250 leads (650/20%)**

- ✔ ***Question:*** What is ABC Association's Gap?
- ✔ ***Answer:*** **Subtract the departure numbers from the destination numbers**

Here are ABC's updated templates showing destination and gap numbers.

Conversion Rate Template			
Conversion Measurements	**Departure**	**Gap**	**Destination**
Leads	0	325	3250
Conversion Rate	10%	10%	20%
New Members	0	650	650

Retention Rate Template			
Retention Measurements	Departure	Gap	Destination
Members	4500	650	4700
Retention Rate	86%	4%	90%

Now it's your turn to answer some questions and determine your destination numbers and gap. You will transfer your answers onto the charts on the following page.

- ✔ ***Question:*** How many members does your association want to have in the next 12 months?
- ✔ ***Answer:*** ___________ **Members**

- ✔ ***Question:*** What is your desired retention rate in the next 12 months?
- ✔ ***Answer:*** ___________ %

- ✔ ***Question:*** How many new members does your association need to have in the next 12 months?
- ✔ ***Answer:*** ___________ **New Members (Destination number – (destination retention rate % x departure membership number)**

- ✔ ***Question:*** What is your desired conversion rate in the next 12 months?
- ✔ ***Answer:*** ___________ %

- ✔ ***Question:*** How many leads does your organization need in the next 12 months?
- ✔ ***Answer:*** ___________ **(Number of new members divided by destination conversion rate)**

- ✔ ***Question:*** What is your Gap?
- ✔ ***Answer:*** **Subtract the departure numbers from the destination numbers.**

Conversion Rate Template			
Conversion Measurements	**Departure**	**Gap**	**Destination**
Leads			
Conversion Rate			
New Members			

Retention Rate Template			
Retention Measurements	Departure	Gap	Destination
Members			
Retention Rate			

Mapping Step 3: Develop Your Map

To develop a map for your organization, we need to again ask and answer some questions following ABC Association's example.

Question: What percentage of leads does ABC want to generate in Q1, Q2, Q3, Q4 respectively to close the gap? Q stands for quarter or 13 weeks.

- ✔ ***Answer:*** **Q1 – 10%, Q2 – 20%, Q3 – 30%, Q – 40%. This will enable ABC to build momentum.**

- ✔ ***Question:*** *What conversion rate will ABC use in the next 12 months as a benchmark to close the gap?*
- ✔ ***Answer:*** **20%. To keep it simple, ABC will use 20% throughout the 4 quarters.**

- ✔ ***Question:*** *What retention rate will ABC use in the next 12 months as a benchmark to close the gap?*
- ✔ ***Answer:*** **95%. To keep it simple, ABC will use 95% throughout the 4 quarters.**

Here is ABC's map:

ABC's New Members Map In Quarters						
Measures	Departure	Q1	Q2	Q3	Q4	Destination
Leads	0	325	650	975	1300	3250
Conversion Rate	0%	20%	20%	20%	20%	20%
New Members	0	65	130	195	260	650
Percentage	0%	10%	20%	30%	40%	100%

Based on the above map, ABC's new membership budget for each quarter on a weekly basis will be as follows:

ABC's New Members Map In Weeks					
Measures	Q1	Q2	Q3	Q4	Total
Leads Per Week	25	50	75	100	3250
Conversion Rate Per Week	20%	20%	20%	20%	20%
New Members Per Week	5	10	15	20	650

To calculate the weekly budget numbers, simply divide the total number of leads for each quarter by 13 weeks as follows:

- 325 leads/13 weeks = 25 leads per week
- 650 leads/13 weeks = 50 leads per week
- 975 leads/13 weeks = 75 leads per week
- 1300 leads/13 weeks = 100 leads per week

Now it's your turn to answer some questions and develop your membership map using the template provided below. You will transfer your answers onto the charts on the following page.

- ✔ *Question:* What percentage of leads does your organization want to generate in Q1, Q2, Q3, Q4 respectively? Even if you are not at the beginning of a quarter, think about the next 13 weeks and plan accordingly.
- ✔ *Answer:* Q1 _____%, Q2 _____ %, Q3 _____%, Q4 _____ %. Enter your answers in the percentage row below.

- ✔ ***Question:*** *What is your organization's projected conversion rate in the next 12 months?*
- ✔ ***Answer:*** _______%. Enter the same rate on the conversion row across the four quarters.
- ✔ ***Question:*** What retention rate is your organization projected to have in the next 12 months?
- ✔ ***Answer:*** _______%. We will be using this retention rate as we calculate and track your membership retention throughout the year.

Here Is Your Organization's New Membership Map Template:

Your New Members Map In Quarters						
Measures	Departure	Q1	Q2	Q3	Q4	Destination
Leads	0					
Conversion	0%					
New Members	0					
Percentage	0%					100%

Divide each quarter's lead numbers by 13 to arrive at your weekly budget. We will be using your weekly new membership budget to track your progress using the accountability scoreboard described in Major Step 4 later on.

Your New Members Map In Weeks					
Measures	Q1	Q2	Q3	Q4	Total
Leads Per Week					
Conversion Rate Per Week					
New Members Per Week					

Now that you have successfully completed your new membership map and know exactly which numbers to focus on each quarter, let's proceed to the next major step to design your content blueprint and calendar.

Major Step 2: Design Your Content Blueprints

There are three types of content we will focus on so your organization can retain more members, convert more leads into members and add more qualified leads into your follow up funnel.

The three types of content are:

1. **Retention Content** – This content is for your current members. When your organization feeds its members with valuable, nutritious content, they will stick around and not cancel their membership.
2. **Conversion Content** – This is your follow up or nurturing content. Without a good follow up sequence and touchpoints, your association will not be able to convert qualified leads into members. When a prospect or future member contacts your organization about joining, only 3 percent of them are actually ready to join and buy a membership. The rest – an overwhelming 97 percent – have to be nurtured along the joining process.
3. **Lead Generation Content** – This is your front-end content. It is like the appetizer that attracts qualified leads. This content has to add value to be attractive to prospective members.

Let's start with your retention content blueprint using some examples.

Retention Content Blueprint

The completed template below is Profitable Content Menu's (PCM) retention content blueprint. We plan to send and provide:

- A **daily tip** to our current members to inspire them so they can keep the momentum up.
- Valuable content **weekly via email** to help our members to increase their retention rate.
- More in-depth valuable content via a **monthly email newsletter** to help our members grow sustainable associations and businesses.
- A practical application **workshop online and/or offline** quarterly to help our members learn and apply new skills so they can grow their associations or businesses.
- An **annual meeting online or offline** to help our members prepare for the following year.

To summarize, here is what Profitable Content Menu's Retention Content looks like:

Our Retention Content Blueprint				
Daily	Weekly	Monthly	Quarterly	Yearly
Tip	Email	Email newsletter	Workshop	Annual Meeting

EXERCISE

Please answer the following questions and enter your answers in your retention content blueprint template provided below (refer back to Step 2, on page 13):

What type of content plate will you use to provide **daily** valuable content to your members?

What type of content plate will you use to provide **weekly** valuable content to your members?

What type of content plate will you use to provide **monthly** valuable content to your members?

What type of content plate will you use to provide **quarterly** valuable content to your members?

What type of content plate will you use to provide **yearly** valuable content to your members?

Transfer your answers from above to the table below.

Your Retention Content Blueprint				
Daily	Weekly	Monthly	Quarterly	Yearly

Retention Content Calendar Blueprint

We plan to send or provide the content above as follows:

Our Retention Content Calendar Blueprint				
Daily	**Weekly**	**Monthly**	**Quarterly**	**Yearly**
M-F 8:00 AM	Thurs @ 2pm	Thurs @ 2 pm: 2nd week of the month	March 15 June 15 Sept 15 Nov 15	Dec. 5

EXERCISE

Please answer the following questions and enter your answers in your retention content calendar blueprint template provided below:

What time and days of the week will your organization provide your **daily** content?

___

What time and day of the week will your organization provide your **weekly** content?

___

What time, day and week of the month will your organization provide your **monthly** content?

___

What date and month of the quarter will your organization provide your **quarterly** content?

___

What date and month of the year will your organization provide your **yearly** content?

___

Your Retention Content Calendar Blueprint				
Daily	**Weekly**	**Monthly**	**Quarterly**	**Yearly**

Now, transfer your above answers for your Retention Content calendar to your electronic calendar. Think of this as your publishing date for your content. For example, I use Google Calendar so I would transfer each one of my content publish dates to the designated days, weeks, months, quarters and annual date on my Google Calendar.

Conversion Content Blueprint

The completed template below is our conversion content blueprint. As you'll recall from earlier in the workbook on page 45, your Conversion Content is your follow up or nurturing content. Without a good follow up sequence and touchpoints, your association will not be able to convert qualified leads into members.

Profitable Content Menu plans to send and provide:

- 8 Follow up emails over a period of two weeks when a qualified lead enters into our follow up funnel.
- Valuable content weekly via email to keep nurturing leads so we can increase our conversion rate.
- More in-depth valuable content via an email newsletter to help our prospects solve specific problems.
- A practical application workshop online and/or offline to help our prospect with specific problems they are encountering.
- An annual workshop focused on planning.

So, here's what Profitable Content Menu's Conversion Content calendar looks like:

Our Conversion Content Blueprint				
Join Funnel	**Weekly**	**Monthly**	**Quarterly**	**Yearly**
8 Emails	**Email**	**Email newsletter**	**Webinar**	**Annual Workshop**

EXERCISE

Please answer the following questions and enter your answers in your conversion content blueprint template provided below:

What type of **content plate** will you use to provide valuable content when leads join your follow up funnel?

What type of content plate will you use to provide **weekly** valuable content to your leads?

What type of content plate will you use to provide **monthly** valuable content to your leads?

What type of content plate will you use to provide **quarterly** valuable content to your leads?

What type of content plate will you use to provide **yearly** valuable content to your leads?

Your Conversion Content Blueprint				
Join Funnel	Weekly	Monthly	Quarterly	Yearly

Conversion Content Calendar Blueprint

We plan to send or provide the content above as follows:

Our Conversion Content Calendar Blueprint				
Join Funnel	Weekly	Monthly	Quarterly	Yearly
1st 14 Days	Thurs @ 2pm	Thurs @ 2 pm: 2nd week of month	March 15 June 15 Sept 15 Nov 15	Dec. 5

EXERCISE

Please answer the following questions and enter your answers in your conversion content calendar blueprint template provided below:

How **long** will your initial follow up campaign last when leads join your follow up funnel?

____

What time and day of the week will your organization provide your **weekly** follow up content?

____

What time, day and week of the month will your organization provide your **monthly** follow up content?

____

What date and month of the quarter will your organization send your **quarterly** follow up content?

____

What date and month of the year will your organization provide your **yearly** follow up content?

____

Your Conversion Content Calendar Blueprint				
Join Funnel	Weekly	Monthly	Quarterly	Yearly

Transfer your answers to create your conversion content calendar electronically. Scheduling time ensures you don't forget and stay focused.

Leads Content Blueprint

The completed template below is Profitable Content Menu's lead generation content blueprint. Along with providing a freebie booklet of costly mistakes that associations make, we also plan to provide:

- **Tips via social media daily.** These tips are designed to add value to our ideal prospects. We also use various lead magnets to attract qualified leads to join our follow up funnel.
- **Valuable content weekly via blog posts.** Each blog post will have a call to action designed to help the prospect advance their journey and join our follow up funnel.
- **Valuable content via our monthly webinar to help our prospects solve specific problems so they can advance their journey and join our follow up funnel.**
- **Valuable testimonials through our quarterly celebration event where we celebrate the success of our members.** The prospects who respond to this invitation become a part of our follow up funnel.
- **An annual profitable content planning event to help our prospects sample a profitable content map.** The prospects who respond to this invitation become a part of our follow up funnel.

Our Lead Generation Content Blueprint				
Daily	Weekly	Monthly	Quarterly	Yearly
Tips	Blog Post	Webinar	Celebration	Content Planning

EXERCISE

Please answer the following questions and enter your answers in your lead generation content blueprint template provided below:

What type of lead magnet (or valuable freebie) will you use to attract qualified leads to join your follow up funnel?

What type of content plate will you use to provide **daily** valuable content to attracts leads?

What type of content plate will you use to provide **weekly** valuable content to attract leads to join your follow up funnel?

What type of content plate will you use to provide **monthly** valuable content to attract leads?

What type of content plate will you use to provide **quarterly** valuable content to attract leads?

What type of content plate will you use to provide **yearly** valuable content to attract your ideal leads?

Your Lead Generation Content Blueprint				
Daily	Weekly	Monthly	Quarterly	Yearly

Lead Generation Content Calendar Blueprint

We plan to send or provide the content above as follows:

Our Lead Generation Content Calendar Blueprint				
Daily	Weekly	Monthly	Quarterly	Yearly
8:00 am M-F	Thurs @ 2pm	Thurs @ 2 pm: Second week of the month	March 15 June 15 Sept. 15 Nov. 15	Dec. 5

EXERCISE

Please answer the following questions and enter your answers in your lead generation content calendar blueprint template provided below:

What time and days of the week will your organization provide your **daily** lead generation content?

What time and day of the week will your organization provide your **weekly** lead generation content?

What time, day and week of the month will your organization provide your **monthly** lead generation content?

What date and month of the quarter will your organization send your **quarterly** lead generation content?

What date and month of the year will your organization provide your **yearly** lead generation content?

Your Lead Generation Content Calendar Blueprint				
Daily	Weekly	Monthly	Quarterly	Yearly

Transfer your answers on when you will schedule your conversion/lead generation content to your electronic calendar.

Major Step 3: Design Your Content Creation Calendar

Many associations have not yet invested the time to create quality retention, conversion and lead generation content. Even if your association has created these three types of content, you still need to keep the content fresh with relevant and timely topics.

If something is not on the calendar, it's hard to get it done. Here is a content creation time investment template below to schedule content creation into your calendar following our example.

Our Content Creation Time Investment Budget					
	Daily	Weekly	Monthly	Quarterly	Yearly
1.Retention	**30 minutes**	**150 minutes**	**10 hours**	**1.25 days**	**5 days**
2.Conversion	**15 minutes**	**75 minutes**	**5 hours**	**15 hours**	**2.5 days**
3.Leads	**15 minutes**	**75 minutes**	**5 hours**	**15 hours**	**2.5 days**

EXERCISE

How much time will your association invest daily, weekly, monthly, quarterly and yearly to create content? Enter your answers in the table below:

Your Content Creation Time Investment Budget					
	Daily	Weekly	Monthly	Quarterly	Yearly
1.Retention					
2.Conversion					
3.Leads					

Major Step 4: Develop Accountability Scoreboards

It is very difficult to track your progress without a scorecard. Unfortunately, many associations and businesses are playing without a scoreboard to measure and celebrate their progress.

This workbook shows you how to develop and use three types of scoreboards so you can stay on track

towards getting new members and keeping more of them for a longer period of time.
The three types of scoreboards are:

- Daily Consistency Rate
- Weekly Conversion Rate
- Quarterly Retention Rate

You can easily know if your association or business will reach its goals by focusing on your consistency rate.

What is a consistency rate?

Consistency rate is the actual time divided by budgeted time. In Step 3 above, you budgeted time to create and provide valuable retention, conversion and lead generation content. Your consistency rate will help you to know how committed your organization is to actually creating and providing the content.

For example, if a member of your team budgets 60 minutes to create retention content on Monday and schedules the 60 minutes on the calendar in advance and follows through, the consistency rate for retention content creation is 100% (60/60). However, if the team member was distracted and only invested 50 minutes, the consistency rate will be 83% (50/60).

How To Calculate Consistency Rate

The table below reflects the daily and weekly content creation time investment budget created in Step 3 above.

Profitable Content	Monday	Tuesday	Wednesday	Thursday	Friday	Weekly Total
Retention	60	60	60	60	60	300
Conversion	60	60	120	60	60	360
Leads	60	60	60	60	120	360
Daily/ Weekly Total	180	180	240	180	240	1020

Assuming that the following actual time was invested each day to create content, the consistency rate for each day and the average for the week will be as follows:

Profitable Content	Monday	Tuesday	Wednesday	Thursday	Friday	Weekly
Budget (B)	180	180	240	180	240	1020
Actual (A)	180	180	200	180	120	860
Consistency Rate: A/B	100%	100%	83%	100%	50%	87%

Based on the above, the weekly consistency rate average is 87%. A consistency rate less than 80% in a week is a sign that your association or business is getting off track.

Weekly Conversion Rate

Conversion Rate is simply a measure of the number of new members divided by the number of leads actually generated expressed as a percentage.

In Major Step 1 above, we were able to develop ABC's weekly map as follows:

ABC's New Members Map In Weeks					
Measures	Q1	Q2	Q3	Q4	Total
Leads Per Week	25	50	75	100	3250
Conversion Rate Per Week	20%	20%	20%	20%	20%
New Members Per Week	5	10	15	20	650

If ABC Association generates 20 leads and converts 15% of them in week 1 of Q1, the weekly accountability conversion rate scoreboard will look like this:

Q1: Week 1 Ending: 9/18/20 Weekly Conversion Rate Scoreboard				
Measures	QTD Budget	QTD Actual	Variance	Progress %
Leads	25	20	(5)	80%
Conversion Rate	20%	15%	(5)	75%
New Members	5	3	(2)	60%

Weekly Conversion Rate Scorecard Interpretation Table	
Variance	QTD Actual Minus QTD Budget
80% to 100%+ Progress	Green
60% to 79% Progress	Yellow
Less Than 60% Progress	Red

These colors enable organizations to determine quickly how a measure is doing. Green shows strong progress and that you're on track to meet budget. Yellow is fair to good progress, and red indicates that you may not be on track to meet your budgetary goals. Weekly scoreboard templates will be provided in the scoreboard templates section of this planner to help your organization keep score weekly.

Quarterly Retention Rate

Quarterly retention rates will enable your organization to determine how your retention content is performing.

To calculate your organization's retention rate at the end of each quarter, take the following steps:

Step 1: Identify the number of members at the beginning of the quarter

Step 2: Identify the number of new members who were added during the quarter

Step 3: Identify the number of members at the end of the quarter

Step 4: Calculate the retention number by subtracting new members number from end of quarter number.

Step 5: Calculate the retention rate by dividing the retention number calculated in step 4 by the beginning number.

ABC Association Example:

Here are the five steps using ABC Association's projected membership numbers:

Step 1: Q1 Beginning number: 4500

Step 2: Q1 New members addition 60

Step 3: Q1 Ending number: 4000

Step 4: Q1 Retention number: 4000 – 60 = 3940

Step 5: Q1 Retention rate: 3940/4500 = 88%

Based on ABC Association's budgeted retention rate of 90%, the retention rate scoreboard will look as follows:

Q1:Ending: 12/31/20 Quarterly Retention Rate Scoreboard				
Measure	**QTD Budget**	**QTD Actual**	**Variance**	**Progress %**
Retention Rate	90%	88%	(2)	98%

Quarterly Retention Rate Scoreboard Interpretation Table	
Variance	**QTD Actual Minus QTD Budget**
90% to 100%+ Progress*	**Green**
70% to 89% Progress	**Yellow**
Less Than 70% Progress	**Red**

* The Retention Rate reflected in Green indicates strong progress. A 90-100 percent Progress Rate is slightly higher than the 80-100 percent Progress Rate for the Conversion Rate. Because Retention Rate measures current membership and Conversion Rate measures those who are not members, we allowed greater leeway for Conversion Rate since it's more difficult to capture new members.

Accountability Meetings

It is recommended that your association schedules and holds the following accountability meetings:

- **Weekly accountability meetings** to review the previous week's conversion rate scoreboard and plan for the following week. These weekly meetings should be held on the same day of the week at the same time to make them habitual. These weekly meetings should be 30 minutes or less.
- **Quarterly accountability meetings** to review the previous quarter's retention rate scoreboard and plan for the following quarter. These quarterly meetings should be held during the first week of a new quarter to review the previous quarter or 13 weeks and plan for the following quarter or 13 weeks. These weekly meetings should be 60 minutes or less.
- **Yearly accountability meetings** to review the current year's cumulative scores and plan for the following year. These yearly meetings should be held towards the end of the 4th quarter. The recommended duration of this meeting is 120 minutes or less.

ACCOUNTABILITY SCOREBOARD TEMPLATES

Daily Consistency Rate Example.

The template below reflects ABC Association's daily and weekly content creation time investment budget created in major step 3 above.

Start Date: Monday 1/4/21

End Date : Friday 1/8/21

Week's Budget In Minutes						
Profitable Content	**Mon**	**Tue**	**Wed**	**Thu**	**Fri**	**Weekly Total**
Retention	60	60	60	60	60	300
Conversion	60	60	120	60	60	360
Leads	60	60	60	60	120	360
Daily/Weekly Total	180	180	240	180	240	1020

Assuming that the following actual time was invested each day to create content, the consistency rate for each day and the average for the week will be as follows:

Week's Daily Consistency Rate And Week's Average						
Profitable Content	**Mon**	**Tue**	**Wed**	**Thu**	**Fri**	**Weekly**
Budget (B)	180	180	240	180	240	1020
Actual (A)	180	180	200	180	120	860
Consistency Rate: A/B	100%	100%	83%	100%	50%	87%

Daily Consistency Rate Scoreboard Templates

Q1. Week 1

What are the week's start and end dates? Enter your answers in the spaces provided.

Start Date: Monday ____________

End Date : Friday ______________

How many minutes have been budgeted in your electronic calendar for each profitable content category each day? Enter your answers in minutes in the template below.

Week's Budget In Minutes						
Profitable Content	**Mon**	**Tue**	**Wed**	**Thu**	**Fri**	**Week Total**
Retention						
Conversion						
Leads						
Daily/Weekly Total						

Enter the total budgeted minutes and the total actual minutes in the template below. We recommend using two electronic calendars. One to budget and the other one for actual so it is easy to calculate the totals at the end of each day and week.

Week's Daily Consistency Rate And Week's Average						
Profitable Content	**Mon**	**Tue**	**Wed**	**Thu**	**Fri**	**Week Average**
Budget (B)						
Actual (A)						
Consistency Rate: A/B						

A weekly average consistency rate of less than 80% is a sign your association's profitable content creation and delivery is getting off track. If nothing is done to get back on track, it will be difficult to achieve your leads, conversion and retention rate goals.

Q1. Week 2

What are the week's start and end dates? Enter your answers in the spaces provided.

Start Date: Monday ____________

End Date : Friday ______________

How many minutes have been budgeted in your electronic calendar for each profitable content category each day? Enter your answers in minutes in the template below.

Week's Budget In Minutes						
Profitable Content	**Mon**	**Tue**	**Wed**	**Thu**	**Fri**	**Week Total**
Retention						
Conversion						
Leads						
Daily/Weekly Total						

Enter the total budgeted minutes and the total actual minutes in the template below. We recommend using two electronic calendars. One to budget and the other one for actual so it is easy to calculate the totals at the end of each day and week.

Week's Daily Consistency Rate And Week's Average						
Profitable Content	**Mon**	**Tue**	**Wed**	**Thu**	**Fri**	**Week Average**
Budget (B)						
Actual (A)						
Consistency Rate: A/B						

A weekly average consistency rate of less than 80% is a sign your association's profitable content creation and delivery is getting off track. If nothing is done to get back on track, it will be very difficult to achieve your leads, conversion and retention rate goals.

Q1. Week 3

What are the week's start and end dates? Enter your answers in the spaces provided.

Start Date: Monday ____________

End Date : Friday ______________

How many minutes have been budgeted in your electronic calendar for each profitable content category each day? Enter your answers in minutes in the template below.

Week's Budget In Minutes						
Profitable Content	**Mon**	**Tue**	**Wed**	**Thu**	**Fri**	**Week Total**
Retention						
Conversion						
Leads						
Daily/Weekly Total						

Enter the total budgeted minutes and the total actual minutes in the template below. We recommend using two electronic calendars. One to budget and the other one for actual so it is easy to calculate the totals at the end of each day and week.

Week's Daily Consistency Rate And Week's Average						
Profitable Content	**Mon**	**Tue**	**Wed**	**Thu**	**Fri**	**Week Average**
Budget (B)						
Actual (A)						
Consistency Rate: A/B						

A weekly average consistency rate of less than 80% is a sign your association's profitable content creation and delivery is getting off track. If nothing is done to get back on track, it will be very difficult to achieve your leads, conversion and retention rate goals.

Q1. Week 4

What are the week's start and end dates? Enter your answers in the spaces provided.

Start Date: Monday ____________

End Date : Friday ____________

How many minutes have been budgeted in your electronic calendar for each profitable content category each day? Enter your answers in minutes in the template below

Week's Budget In Minutes						
Profitable Content	**Mon**	**Tue**	**Wed**	**Thu**	**Fri**	**Week Total**
Retention						
Conversion						
Leads						
Daily/Weekly Total						

Enter the total budgeted minutes and the total actual minutes in the template below. We recommend using two electronic calendars. One to budget and the other one for actual so it is easy to calculate the totals at the end of each day and week.

Week's Daily Consistency Rate And Week's Average						
Profitable Content	**Mon**	**Tue**	**Wed**	**Thu**	**Fri**	**Week Average**
Budget (B)						
Actual (A)						
Consistency Rate: A/B						

A weekly average consistency rate of less than 80% is a sign your association's profitable content creation and delivery is getting off track. If nothing is done to get back on track, it will be very difficult to achieve your leads, conversion and retention rate goals.

Q1. Week 5

What are the week's start and end dates? Enter your answers in the spaces provided.

Start Date: Monday ____________

End Date : Friday ______________

How many minutes have been budgeted in your electronic calendar for each profitable content category each day? Enter your answers in minutes in the template below.

Week's Budget In Minutes						
Profitable Content	**Mon**	**Tue**	**Wed**	**Thu**	**Fri**	**Week Total**
Retention						
Conversion						
Leads						
Daily/Weekly Total						

Enter the total budgeted minutes and the total actual minutes in the template below. We recommend using two electronic calendars. One to budget and the other one for actual so it is easy to calculate the totals at the end of each day and week.

Week's Daily Consistency Rate And Week's Average						
Profitable Content	**Mon**	**Tue**	**Wed**	**Thu**	**Fri**	**Week Average**
Budget (B)						
Actual (A)						
Consistency Rate: A/B						

A weekly average consistency rate of less than 80% is a sign your association's profitable content creation and delivery is getting off track. If nothing is done to get back on track, it will be very difficult to achieve your leads, conversion and retention rate goals.

Q1. Week 6

What are the week's start and end dates? Enter your answers in the spaces provided.

Start Date: Monday ____________

End Date : Friday ____________

How many minutes have been budgeted in your electronic calendar for each profitable content category each day? Enter your answers in minutes in the template below.

Week's Budget In Minutes						
Profitable Content	**Mon**	**Tue**	**Wed**	**Thu**	**Fri**	**Week Total**
Retention						
Conversion						
Leads						
Daily/Weekly Total						

Enter the total budgeted minutes and the total actual minutes in the template below. We recommend using two electronic calendars. One to budget and the other one for actual so it is easy to calculate the totals at the end of each day and week.

Week's Daily Consistency Rate And Week's Average						
Profitable Content	**Mon**	**Tue**	**Wed**	**Thu**	**Fri**	**Week Average**
Budget (B)						
Actual (A)						
Consistency Rate: A/B						

A weekly average consistency rate of less than 80% is a sign your association's profitable content creation and delivery is getting off track. If nothing is done to get back on track, it will be very difficult to achieve your leads, conversion and retention rate goals.

Q1. Week 7

What are the week's start and end dates? Enter your answers in the spaces provided.

Start Date: Monday ____________

End Date : Friday ______________

How many minutes have been budgeted in your electronic calendar for each profitable content category each day? Enter your answers in minutes in the template below.

Week's Budget In Minutes						
Profitable Content	**Mon**	**Tue**	**Wed**	**Thu**	**Fri**	**Week Total**
Retention						
Conversion						
Leads						
Daily/Weekly Total						

Enter the total budgeted minutes and the total actual minutes in the template below. We recommend using two electronic calendars. One to budget and the other one for actual so it is easy to calculate the totals at the end of each day and week.

Week's Daily Consistency Rate And Week's Average						
Profitable Content	**Mon**	**Tue**	**Wed**	**Thu**	**Fri**	**Week Average**
Budget (B)						
Actual (A)						
Consistency Rate: A/B						

A weekly average consistency rate of less than 80% is a sign your association's profitable content creation and delivery is getting off track. If nothing is done to get back on track, it will be very difficult to achieve your leads, conversion and retention rate goals.

Q1. Week 8

What are the week's start and end dates? Enter your answers in the spaces provided.

Start Date: Monday ____________

End Date : Friday ______________

How many minutes have been budgeted in your electronic calendar for each profitable content category each day? Enter your answers in minutes in the template below.

Week's Budget In Minutes						
Profitable Content	**Mon**	**Tue**	**Wed**	**Thu**	**Fri**	**Week Total**
Retention						
Conversion						
Leads						
Daily/Weekly Total						

Enter the total budgeted minutes and the total actual minutes in the template below. We recommend using two electronic calendars. One to budget and the other one for actual so it is easy to calculate the totals at the end of each day and week.

Week's Daily Consistency Rate And Week's Average						
Profitable Content	**Mon**	**Tue**	**Wed**	**Thu**	**Fri**	**Week Average**
Budget (B)						
Actual (A)						
Consistency Rate: A/B						

A weekly average consistency rate of less than 80% is a sign your association's profitable content creation and delivery is getting off track. If nothing is done to get back on track, it will be very difficult to achieve your leads, conversion and retention rate goals.

Q1. Week 9

What are the week's start and end dates? Enter your answers in the spaces provided.

Start Date: Monday ____________

End Date : Friday ______________

How many minutes have been budgeted in your electronic calendar for each profitable content category each day? Enter your answers in minutes in the template below.

Week's Budget In Minutes						
Profitable Content	**Mon**	**Tue**	**Wed**	**Thu**	**Fri**	**Week Total**
Retention						
Conversion						
Leads						
Daily/Weekly Total						

Enter the total budgeted minutes and the total actual minutes in the template below. We recommend using two electronic calendars. One to budget and the other one for actual so it is easy to calculate the totals at the end of each day and week.

Week's Daily Consistency Rate And Week's Average						
Profitable Content	**Mon**	**Tue**	**Wed**	**Thu**	**Fri**	**Week Average**
Budget (B)						
Actual (A)						
Consistency Rate: A/B						

A weekly average consistency rate of less than 80% is a sign your association's profitable content creation and delivery is getting off track. If nothing is done to get back on track, it will be very difficult to achieve your leads, conversion and retention rate goals.

Q1. Week 10

What are the week's start and end dates? Enter your answers in the spaces provided.

Start Date: Monday ______________

End Date : Friday ________________

How many minutes have been budgeted in your electronic calendar for each profitable content category each day? Enter your answers in minutes in the template below.

Week's Budget In Minutes						
Profitable Content	**Mon**	**Tue**	**Wed**	**Thu**	**Fri**	**Week Total**
Retention						
Conversion						
Leads						
Daily/Weekly Total						

Enter the total budgeted minutes and the total actual minutes in the template below. We recommend using two electronic calendars. One to budget and the other one for actual so it is easy to calculate the totals at the end of each day and week.

Week's Daily Consistency Rate And Week's Average						
Profitable Content	**Mon**	**Tue**	**Wed**	**Thu**	**Fri**	**Week Average**
Budget (B)						
Actual (A)						
Consistency Rate: A/B						

A weekly average consistency rate of less than 80% is a sign your association's profitable content creation and delivery is getting off track. If nothing is done to get back on track, it will be very difficult to achieve your leads, conversion and retention rate goals.

Q1. Week 11

What are the week's start and end dates? Enter your answers in the spaces provided.

Start Date: Monday ____________

End Date : Friday ____________

How many minutes have been budgeted in your electronic calendar for each profitable content category each day? Enter your answers in minutes in the template below.

Week's Budget In Minutes						
Profitable Content	**Mon**	**Tue**	**Wed**	**Thu**	**Fri**	**Week Total**
Retention						
Conversion						
Leads						
Daily/Weekly Total						

Enter the total budgeted minutes and the total actual minutes in the template below. We recommend using two electronic calendars. One to budget and the other one for actual so it is easy to calculate the totals at the end of each day and week.

Week's Daily Consistency Rate And Week's Average						
Profitable Content	**Mon**	**Tue**	**Wed**	**Thu**	**Fri**	**Week Average**
Budget (B)						
Actual (A)						
Consistency Rate: A/B						

A weekly average consistency rate of less than 80% is a sign your association's profitable content creation and delivery is getting off track. If nothing is done to get back on track, it will be very difficult to achieve your leads, conversion and retention rate goals.

Q1. Week 12

What are the week's start and end dates? Enter your answers in the spaces provided.

Start Date: Monday ______________

End Date : Friday ______________

How many minutes have been budgeted in your electronic calendar for each profitable content category each day? Enter your answers in minutes in the template below

Week's Budget In Minutes						
Profitable Content	**Mon**	**Tue**	**Wed**	**Thu**	**Fri**	**Week Total**
Retention						
Conversion						
Leads						
Daily/Weekly Total						

Enter the total budgeted minutes and the total actual minutes in the template below. We recommend using two electronic calendars. One to budget and the other one for actual so it is easy to calculate the totals at the end of each day and week.

Week's Daily Consistency Rate And Week's Average						
Profitable Content	**Mon**	**Tue**	**Wed**	**Thu**	**Fri**	**Week Average**
Budget (B)						
Actual (A)						
Consistency Rate: A/B						

A weekly average consistency rate of less than 80% is a sign your association's profitable content creation and delivery is getting off track. If nothing is done to get back on track, it will be very difficult to achieve your leads, conversion and retention rate goals.

Q1. Week 13

What are the week's start and end dates? Enter your answers in the spaces provided.

Start Date: Monday ____________

End Date : Friday ______________

How many minutes have been budgeted in your electronic calendar for each profitable content category each day? Enter your answers in minutes in the template below.

Week's Budget In Minutes						
Profitable Content	Mon	Tue	Wed	Thu	Fri	Week Total
Retention						
Conversion						
Leads						

Enter the total budgeted minutes and the total actual minutes in the template below. We recommend using two electronic calendars. One to budget and the other one for actual so it is easy to calculate the totals at the end of each day and week.

Week's Daily Consistency Rate And Week's Average						
Profitable Content	Mon	Tue	Wed	Thu	Fri	Week Average
Budget (B)						
Actual (A)						
Consistency Rate: A/B						

A weekly average consistency rate of less than 80% is a sign your association's profitable content creation and delivery is getting off track. If nothing is done to get back on track, it will be very difficult to achieve your leads, conversion and retention rate goals.

Weekly Conversion Rate Scoreboard Example

Conversion Rate is simply a measure of the number of new members divided by the number of leads actually generated expressed as a percentage.

In major step 1 above, we were able to develop ABC's weekly map as follows:

ABC's New Members Map In Weeks					
Measures	Q1	Q2	Q3	Q4	Total
Leads Per Week	25	50	75	100	3250
Conversion Rate Per Week	20%	20%	20%	20%	20%
New Members Per Week	5	10	15	20	650

If ABC Association generates 20 leads and converts 15% of them in week 1 of Q1, the weekly accountability conversion rate scoreboard will look like this:

Q1: Week 1 Ending: 9/18/20 Weekly Conversion Rate Scoreboard				
Measures	QTD Budget	QTD Actual	Variance	Progress %
Leads	25	20	(5)	80%
Conversion Rate	20%	15%	(5)	75%
New Members	5	3	(2)	60%

Weekly Conversion Rate Scoreboard Interpretation Table	
Progress	
80% to 100%+ Progress	Green
60% to 79% Progress	Yellow
Less Than 60% Progress	Red

"Variance" is QTD Actual minus QTD Budget

These colors enable organizations to determine quickly how a measure is doing. Weekly scoreboard templates will be provided in the scoreboard templates section of this planner to enable your organization keep score weekly

Weekly Conversion Rate Scoreboard Templates

Enter your association's budget and actual numbers below and calculate the variance and progress %.

Q1: Week 1 Ending: ____________Weekly Conversion Rate Scoreboard				
Measures	QTD Budget	QTD Actual	Variance	Progress %
Leads				
Conversion Rate				
New Members				
Q1: Week 2 Ending: ____________ Weekly Conversion Rate Scoreboard				
Measures	QTD Budget	QTD Actual	Variance	Progress %
Leads				
Conversion Rate				
New Members				

Q1: Week 3 Ending: ___________ Weekly Conversion Rate Scoreboard				
Measures	QTD Budget	QTD Actual	Variance	Progress %
Leads				
Conversion Rate				
New Members				

Q1: Week 4 Ending: ___________ Weekly Conversion Rate Scoreboard				
Measures	QTD Budget	QTD Actual	Variance	Progress %
Leads				
Conversion Rate				
New Members				

Q1: Week 5 Ending: ___________ Weekly Conversion Rate Scoreboard				
Measures	QTD Budget	QTD Actual	Variance	Progress %
Leads				
Conversion Rate				
New Members				

Q1: Week 6 Ending: ___________ Weekly Conversion Rate Scoreboard				
Measures	QTD Budget	QTD Actual	Variance	Progress %
Leads				
Conversion Rate				
New Members				

Q1: Week 7 Ending: ___________ Weekly Conversion Rate Scoreboard				
Measures	QTD Budget	QTD Actual	Variance	Progress %
Leads				
Conversion Rate				
New Members				

Q1: Week 8 Ending: ___________ Weekly Conversion Rate Scoreboard				
Measures	QTD Budget	QTD Actual	Variance	Progress %
Leads				
Conversion Rate				
New Members				

Q1: Week 9 Ending: ___________ Weekly Conversion Rate Scoreboard				
Measures	QTD Budget	QTD Actual	Variance	Progress %
Leads				
Conversion Rate				
New Members				
Q1: Week 10 Ending: ___________ Weekly Conversion Rate Scoreboard				
Measures	QTD Budget	QTD Actual	Variance	Progress %
Leads				
Conversion Rate				
New Members				
Q1: Week 11 Ending: ___________ Weekly Conversion Rate Scoreboard				
Measures	QTD Budget	QTD Actual	Variance	Progress %
Leads				
Conversion Rate				
New Members				
Q1: Week 12 Ending: ___________ Weekly Conversion Rate Scoreboard				
Measures	QTD Budget	QTD Actual	Variance	Progress %
Leads				
Conversion Rate				
New Members				
Q1: Week 13 Ending: ___________ Weekly Conversion Rate Scoreboard				
Measures	QTD Budget	QTD Actual	Variance	Progress %
Leads				
Conversion Rate				
New Members				

Quarterly Retention Rate Example

Quarterly retention rates will enable your organization to determine how your retention content is performing.

To calculate your organization's retention rate at the end of each quarter, take the following steps:

Step 1: Identify the number of members at the beginning of the quarter

Step 2: Identify the number of new members who were added during the quarter

Step 3: Identify the number of members at the end of the quarter

Step 4: Calculate the retention number by subtracting new members number from end of quarter number.

Step 5: Calculate the retention rate by dividing the retention number calculated in step 4 by the beginning number.

ABC Association Example:

Here are the five steps using ABC Association's projected membership numbers:

Step 1: Q1 Beginning number: 4500

Step 2: Q1 New members addition 60

Step 3: Q1 Ending number: 4000

Step 4: Q1 Retention number: 4000 – 60 = 3940

Step 5: Q1 Retention rate: 3940/4500 = 88%

Based on ABC Association's budgeted retention rate of 90%, the retention rate scoreboard will look as follows:

Q1: Ending: 12/31/20 Quarterly Retention Rate Scoreboard				
Measure	QTD Budget	QTD Actual	Variance	Progress %
Retention Rate	90%	88%	(2)	98%

Quarterly Retention Rate Scoreboard Interpretation Table	
Progress	
90% to 100%+ Progress	Green
70% to 89% Progress	Yellow
Less Than 70% Progress	Red

"Variance" is QTD Actual minus QTD Budget

These colors enable organizations to determine quickly how their retention rate is progressing. Quarterly scoreboard templates will be provided in the scoreboard templates section of this planner to enable your organization keep score quarterly.

Quarterly Retention Rate Scoreboard Template

Enter the quarter's ending date and follow the five steps above to calculate your association's retention rate for the quarter and compare it to the budgeted retention rate established in major step 1 above.

Q1: Ending: Quarterly Retention Rate Scoreboard				
Measure	QTD Budget	QTD Actual	Variance	Progress %
Retention Rate				

Daily Consistency Rate Scoreboard Templates

Q2. Week 1

What are the week's start and end dates? Enter your answers in the spaces provided.

Start Date: Monday ____________

End Date : Friday ______________

How many minutes have been budgeted in your electronic calendar for each profitable content category each day? Enter your answers in minutes in the template below.

Week's Budget In Minutes						
Profitable Content	Mon	Tue	Wed	Thu	Fri	Weekly
Retention						
Conversion						
Leads						
Daily/Weekly Total						

Enter the total budgeted minutes and the total actual minutes in the template below. We recommend using two electronic calendars. One to budget and the other one for actual so it is easy to calculate the totals at the end of each day and week.

Week's Daily Consistency Rate And Week's Average						
Profitable Content	Mon	Tue	Wed	Thu	Fri	Weekly
Budget (B)						
Actual (A)						
Consistency Rate: A/B						

A weekly average consistency rate of less than 80% is a sign your association's profitable content creation and delivery is getting off track. If nothing is done to get back on track, it will be very difficult to achieve your leads, conversion and retention rate goals.

Q2. Week 2

What are the week's start and end dates? Enter your answers in the spaces provided.

Start Date: Monday ____________

End Date : Friday ______________

How many minutes have been budgeted in your electronic calendar for each profitable content category each day? Enter your answers in minutes in the template below.

Week's Budget In Minutes						
Profitable Content	**Mon**	**Tue**	**Wed**	**Thu**	**Fri**	**Week Total**
Retention						
Conversion						
Leads						
Daily/Weekly Total						

Enter the total budgeted minutes and the total actual minutes in the template below. We recommend using two electronic calendars. One to budget and the other one for actual so it is easy to calculate the totals at the end of each day and week.

Week's Daily Consistency Rate And Week's Average						
Profitable Content	**Mon**	**Tue**	**Wed**	**Thu**	**Fri**	**Week Average**
Budget (B)						
Actual (A)						
Consistency Rate: A/B						

A weekly average consistency rate of less than 80% is a sign your association's profitable content creation and delivery is getting off track. If nothing is done to get back on track, it will be difficult to achieve your leads, conversion and retention rate goals.

Q2. Week 3

What are the week's start and end dates? Enter your answers in the spaces provided.

Start Date: Monday ____________

End Date : Friday ______________

How many minutes have been budgeted in your electronic calendar for each profitable content category each day? Enter your answers in minutes in the template below.

Week's Budget In Minutes						
Profitable Content	**Mon**	**Tue**	**Wed**	**Thu**	**Fri**	**Week Total**
Retention						
Conversion						
Leads						
Daily/Weekly Total						

Enter the total budgeted minutes and the total actual minutes in the template below. We recommend using two electronic calendars. One to budget and the other one for actual so it is easy to calculate the totals at the end of each day and week.

Week's Daily Consistency Rate And Week's Average						
Profitable Content	**Mon**	**Tue**	**Wed**	**Thu**	**Fri**	**Week Average**
Budget (B)						
Actual (A)						
Consistency Rate: A/B						

A weekly average consistency rate of less than 80% is a sign your association's profitable content creation and delivery is getting off track. If nothing is done to get back on track, it will be very difficult to achieve your leads, conversion and retention rate goals.

Q2. Week 4

What are the week's start and end dates? Enter your answers in the spaces provided.

Start Date: Monday ____________

End Date : Friday ______________

How many minutes have been budgeted in your electronic calendar for each profitable content category each day? Enter your answers in minutes in the template below.

Week's Budget In Minutes						
Profitable Content	**Mon**	**Tue**	**Wed**	**Thu**	**Fri**	**Week Total**
Retention						
Conversion						
Leads						
Daily/Weekly Total						

Enter the total budgeted minutes and the total actual minutes in the template below. We recommend using two electronic calendars. One to budget and the other one for actual so it is easy to calculate the totals at the end of each day and week.

Week's Daily Consistency Rate And Week's Average						
Profitable Content	**Mon**	**Tue**	**Wed**	**Thu**	**Fri**	**Week Average**
Budget (B)						
Actual (A)						
Consistency Rate: A/B						

A weekly average consistency rate of less than 80% is a sign your association's profitable content creation and delivery is getting off track. If nothing is done to get back on track, it will be very difficult to achieve your leads, conversion and retention rate goals.

Q2. Week 5

What are the week's start and end dates? Enter your answers in the spaces provided.

Start Date: Monday ____________

End Date : Friday ____________

How many minutes have been budgeted in your electronic calendar for each profitable content category each day? Enter your answers in minutes in the template below

Week's Budget In Minutes						
Profitable Content	**Mon**	**Tue**	**Wed**	**Thu**	**Fri**	**Week Total**
Retention						
Conversion						
Leads						
Daily/Weekly Total						

Enter the total budgeted minutes and the total actual minutes in the template below. We recommend using two electronic calendars. One to budget and the other one for actual so it is easy to calculate the totals at the end of each day and week.

Week's Daily Consistency Rate And Week's Average						
Profitable Content	**Mon**	**Tue**	**Wed**	**Thu**	**Fri**	**Week Average**
Budget (B)						
Actual (A)						
Consistency Rate: A/B						

A weekly average consistency rate of less than 80% is a sign your association's profitable content creation and delivery is getting off track. If nothing is done to get back on track, it will be very difficult to achieve your leads, conversion and retention rate goals.

Q2. Week 6

What are the week's start and end dates? Enter your answers in the spaces provided.

Start Date: Monday ____________

End Date : Friday ______________

How many minutes have been budgeted in your electronic calendar for each profitable content category each day? Enter your answers in minutes in the template below.

Week's Budget In Minutes						
Profitable Content	**Mon**	**Tue**	**Wed**	**Thu**	**Fri**	**Week Total**
Retention						
Conversion						
Leads						
Daily/Weekly Total						

Enter the total budgeted minutes and the total actual minutes in the template below. We recommend using two electronic calendars. One to budget and the other one for actual so it is easy to calculate the totals at the end of each day and week.

Week's Daily Consistency Rate And Week's Average						
Profitable Content	**Mon**	**Tue**	**Wed**	**Thu**	**Fri**	**Week Average**
Budget (B)						
Actual (A)						
Consistency Rate: A/B						

A weekly average consistency rate of less than 80% is a sign your association's profitable content creation and delivery is getting off track. If nothing is done to get back on track, it will be very difficult to achieve your leads, conversion and retention rate goals.

Q2. Week 7

What are the week's start and end dates? Enter your answers in the spaces provided.

Start Date: Monday ______________

End Date : Friday ________________

How many minutes have been budgeted in your electronic calendar for each profitable content category each day? Enter your answers in minutes in the template below.

Week's Budget In Minutes						
Profitable Content	**Mon**	**Tue**	**Wed**	**Thu**	**Fri**	**Week Total**
Retention						
Conversion						
Leads						
Daily/Weekly Total						

Enter the total budgeted minutes and the total actual minutes in the template below. We recommend using two electronic calendars. One to budget and the other one for actual so it is easy to calculate the totals at the end of each day and week.

Week's Daily Consistency Rate And Week's Average						
Profitable Content	**Mon**	**Tue**	**Wed**	**Thu**	**Fri**	**Week Average**
Budget (B)						
Actual (A)						
Consistency Rate: A/B						

A weekly average consistency rate of less than 80% is a sign your association's profitable content creation and delivery is getting off track. If nothing is done to get back on track, it will be very difficult to achieve your leads, conversion and retention rate goals.

Q2. Week 8

What are the week's start and end dates? Enter your answers in the spaces provided.

Start Date: Monday ____________

End Date : Friday ____________

How many minutes have been budgeted in your electronic calendar for each profitable content category each day? Enter your answers in minutes in the template below.

Week's Budget In Minutes						
Profitable Content	**Mon**	**Tue**	**Wed**	**Thu**	**Fri**	**Week Total**
Retention						
Conversion						
Leads						
Daily/Weekly Total						

Enter the total budgeted minutes and the total actual minutes in the template below. We recommend using two electronic calendars. One to budget and the other one for actual so it is easy to calculate the totals at the end of each day and week.

Week's Daily Consistency Rate And Week's Average						
Profitable Content	**Mon**	**Tue**	**Wed**	**Thu**	**Fri**	**Week Average**
Budget (B)						
Actual (A)						
Consistency Rate: A/B						

A weekly average consistency rate of less than 80% is a sign your association's profitable content creation and delivery is getting off track. If nothing is done to get back on track, it will be very difficult to achieve your leads, conversion and retention rate goals.

Q2. Week 9

What are the week's start and end dates? Enter your answers in the spaces provided.

Start Date: Monday ____________

End Date : Friday ______________

How many minutes have been budgeted in your electronic calendar for each profitable content category each day? Enter your answers in minutes in the template below.

Week's Budget In Minutes						
Profitable Content	**Mon**	**Tue**	**Wed**	**Thu**	**Fri**	**Week Total**
Retention						
Conversion						
Leads						
Daily/Weekly Total						

Enter the total budgeted minutes and the total actual minutes in the template below. We recommend using two electronic calendars. One to budget and the other one for actual so it is easy to calculate the totals at the end of each day and week.

Week's Daily Consistency Rate And Week's Average						
Profitable Content	**Mon**	**Tue**	**Wed**	**Thu**	**Fri**	**Week Average**
Budget (B)						
Actual (A)						
Consistency Rate: A/B						

A weekly average consistency rate of less than 80% is a sign your association's profitable content creation and delivery is getting off track. If nothing is done to get back on track, it will be very difficult to achieve your leads, conversion and retention rate goals.

Q2. Week 10

What are the week's start and end dates? Enter your answers in the spaces provided.

Start Date: Monday ____________

End Date : Friday ______________

How many minutes have been budgeted in your electronic calendar for each profitable content category each day? Enter your answers in minutes in the template below.

Week's Budget In Minutes						
Profitable Content	**Mon**	**Tue**	**Wed**	**Thu**	**Fri**	**Week Total**
Retention						
Conversion						
Leads						
Daily/Weekly Total						

Enter the total budgeted minutes and the total actual minutes in the template below. We recommend using two electronic calendars. One to budget and the other one for actual so it is easy to calculate the totals at the end of each day and week.

Week's Daily Consistency Rate And Week's Average						
Profitable Content	**Mon**	**Tue**	**Wed**	**Thu**	**Fri**	**Week Average**
Budget (B)						
Actual (A)						
Consistency Rate: A/B						

A weekly average consistency rate of less than 80% is a sign your association's profitable content creation and delivery is getting off track. If nothing is done to get back on track, it will be very difficult to achieve your leads, conversion and retention rate goals.

Q2. Week 11

What are the week's start and end dates? Enter your answers in the spaces provided.

Start Date: Monday _____________

End Date : Friday _______________

How many minutes have been budgeted in your electronic calendar for each profitable content category each day? Enter your answers in minutes in the template below.

Week's Budget In Minutes						
Profitable Content	Mon	Tue	Wed	Thu	Fri	Week Total
Retention						
Conversion						
Leads						
Daily/Weekly Total						

Enter the total budgeted minutes and the total actual minutes in the template below. We recommend using two electronic calendars. One to budget and the other one for actual so it is easy to calculate the totals at the end of each day and week.

Week's Daily Consistency Rate And Week's Average						
Profitable Content	Mon	Tue	Wed	Thu	Fri	Week Average
Budget (B)						
Actual (A)						
Consistency Rate: A/B						

A weekly average consistency rate of less than 80% is a sign your association's profitable content creation and delivery is getting off track. If nothing is done to get back on track, it will be very difficult to achieve your leads, conversion and retention rate goals.

Q2. Week 12

What are the week's start and end dates? Enter your answers in the spaces provided.

Start Date: Monday ____________

End Date : Friday ______________

How many minutes have been budgeted in your electronic calendar for each profitable content category each day? Enter your answers in minutes in the template below.

Week's Budget In Minutes						
Profitable Content	**Mon**	**Tue**	**Wed**	**Thu**	**Fri**	**Week Total**
Retention						
Conversion						
Leads						
Daily/Weekly Total						

Enter the total budgeted minutes and the total actual minutes in the template below. We recommend using two electronic calendars. One to budget and the other one for actual so it is easy to calculate the totals at the end of each day and week.

Week's Daily Consistency Rate And Week's Average						
Profitable Content	**Mon**	**Tue**	**Wed**	**Thu**	**Fri**	**Week Average**
Budget (B)						
Actual (A)						
Consistency Rate: A/B						

A weekly average consistency rate of less than 80% is a sign your association's profitable content creation and delivery is getting off track. If nothing is done to get back on track, it will be very difficult to achieve your leads, conversion and retention rate goals.

Q2. Week 13

What are the week's start and end dates? Enter your answers in the spaces provided.

Start Date: Monday ____________

End Date : Friday ______________

How many minutes have been budgeted in your electronic calendar for each profitable content category each day? Enter your answers in minutes in the template below.

Week's Budget In Minutes						
Profitable Content	**Mon**	**Tue**	**Wed**	**Thu**	**Fri**	**Week Total**
Retention						
Conversion						
Leads						
Daily/Weekly Total						

Enter the total budgeted minutes and the total actual minutes in the template below. We recommend using two electronic calendars. One to budget and the other one for actual so it is easy to calculate the totals at the end of each day and week.

Week's Daily Consistency Rate And Week's Average						
Profitable Content	**Mon**	**Tue**	**Wed**	**Thu**	**Fri**	**Week Average**
Budget (B)						
Actual (A)						
Consistency Rate: A/B						

A weekly average consistency rate of less than 80% is a sign your association's profitable content creation and delivery is getting off track. If nothing is done to get back on track, it will be very difficult to achieve your leads, conversion and retention rate goals.

Weekly Conversion Rate Scoreboard Example

Conversion Rate is simply a measure of the number of new members divided by the number of leads actually generated expressed as a percentage.

In major step 1 above, we were able to develop ABC's weekly map as follows:

ABC's New Members Map In Weeks					
Measures	**Q2**	**Q2**	**Q3**	**Q4**	**Total**
Leads Per Week	25	50	75	100	3250
Conversion Rate Per Week	20%	20%	20%	20%	20%
New Members Per Week	5	10	15	20	650

If ABC Association generates 20 leads and converts 15% of them in week 1 of Q2, the weekly accountability conversion rate scoreboard will look like this:

Q2: Week 1 Ending: 9/18/20 Weekly Conversion Rate Scoreboard				
Measures	QTD Budget	QTD Actual	Variance	Progress %
Leads	25	20	(5)	80%
Conversion Rate	20%	15%	(5)	75%
New Members	5	3	(2)	60%

Weekly Conversion Rate Scoreboard Interpretation Table	
Progress	
80% to 100%+ Progress	Green
60% to 79% Progress	Yellow
Less Than 60% Progress	Red

"Variance" is QTD Actual minus QTD Budget

These colors enable organizations to determine quickly how a measure is doing. Weekly scoreboard templates will be provided in the scoreboard templates section of this planner to enable your organization keep score weekly

Weekly Conversion Rate Scoreboard Templates

Enter your association's budget and actual numbers below and calculate the variance and progress %.

Q2: Week 1 Ending ___________Weekly Conversion Rate Scoreboard				
Measures	QTD Budget	QTD Actual	Variance	Progress %
Leads				
Conversion Rate				
New Members				
Q2: Week 2 Ending: ___________ Weekly Conversion Rate Scoreboard				
Measures	QTD Budget	QTD Actual	Variance	Progress %
Leads				
Conversion Rate				
New Members				

Q2: Week 3 Ending: __________Weekly Conversion Rate Scoreboard				
Measures	QTD Budget	QTD Actual	Variance	Progress %
Leads				
Conversion Rate				
New Members				

Q2: Week 4 Ending:__________Weekly Conversion Rate Scoreboard				
Measures	QTD Budget	QTD Actual	Variance	Progress %
Leads				
Conversion Rate				
New Members				

Q2: Week 5 Ending:__________Weekly Conversion Rate Scoreboard				
Measures	QTD Budget	QTD Actual	Variance	Progress %
Leads				
Conversion Rate				
New Members				

Q2: Week 6 Ending: __________ Weekly Conversion Rate Scoreboard				
Measures	QTD Budget	QTD Actual	Variance	Progress %
Leads				
Conversion Rate				
New Members				

Q2: Week 7 Ending: __________Weekly Conversion Rate Scoreboard				
Measures	QTD Budget	QTD Actual	Variance	Progress %
Leads				
Conversion Rate				
New Members				

Q2: Week 8 Ending: __________ Weekly Conversion Rate Scoreboard				
Measures	QTD Budget	QTD Actual	Variance	Progress %
Leads				
Conversion Rate				
New Members				

Q2: Week 9 Ending: ___________ Weekly Conversion Rate Scoreboard				
Measures	QTD Budget	QTD Actual	Variance	Progress %
Leads				
Conversion Rate				
New Members				

Q2: Week 10 Ending: ___________ Weekly Conversion Rate Scoreboard				
Measures	QTD Budget	QTD Actual	Variance	Progress %
Leads				
Conversion Rate				
New Members				

Q2: Week 11 Ending: ___________ Weekly Conversion Rate Scoreboard				
Measures	QTD Budget	QTD Actual	Variance	Progress %
Leads				
Conversion Rate				
New Members				

Q2: Week 12 Ending: ___________ Weekly Conversion Rate Scoreboard				
Measures	QTD Budget	QTD Actual	Variance	Progress %
Leads				
Conversion Rate				
New Members				

Q2: Week 13 Ending: ___________ Weekly Conversion Rate Scoreboard				
Measures	QTD Budget	QTD Actual	Variance	Progress %
Leads				
Conversion Rate				
New Members				

Quarterly Retention Rate Example

Quarterly retention rates will enable your organization to determine how your retention content is performing.

To calculate your organization's retention rate at the end of each quarter, take the following steps:

Step 1: Identify the number of members at the beginning of the quarter

Step 2: Identify the number of new members who were added during the quarter

Step 3: Identify the number of members at the end of the quarter

Step 4: Calculate the retention number by subtracting new members number from end of quarter number.

Step 5: Calculate the retention rate by dividing the retention number calculated in step 4 by the beginning number.

ABC Association Example:

Here are the five steps using ABC Association's projected membership numbers:

Step 1: Q2 Beginning number: 4500

Step 2: Q2 New members addition 60

Step 3: Q2 Ending number: 4000

Step 4: Q2 Retention number: 4000 – 60 = 3940

Step 5: Q2 Retention rate: 3940/4500 = 88%

Based on ABC Association's budgeted retention rate of 90%, the retention rate scoreboard will look as follows:

Q2: Ending: Quarterly Retention Rate Scoreboard				
Measure	QTD Budget	QTD Actual	Variance	Progress %
Retention Rate	90%	88%	(2)	98%

Quarterly Retention Rate Scoreboard Interpretation Table	
Progress	
90% to 100%+ Progress	Green
70% to 89% Progress	Yellow
Less Than 70% Progress	Red

"Variance" is QTD Actual minus QTD Budget

These colors enable organizations to determine quickly how their retention rate is progressing. Quarterly scoreboard templates will be provided in the scoreboard templates section of this planner to enable your organization keep score quarterly.

Quarterly Retention Rate Scoreboard Template

Enter the quarter's ending date and follow the five steps above to calculate your association's retention rate for the quarter and compare it to the budgeted retention rate established in major step 1 above.

Q2: Ending: Quarterly Retention Rate Scoreboard				
Measure	QTD Budget	QTD Actual	Variance	Progress %
Retention Rate				

Daily Consistency Rate Scoreboard Templates

Q3. Week 1

What are the week's start and end dates? Enter your answers in the spaces provided.

Start Date: Monday ____________

End Date : Friday ______________

How many minutes have been budgeted in your electronic calendar for each profitable content category each day? Enter your answers in minutes in the template below.

Week's Budget In Minutes						
Profitable Content	Mon	Tue	Wed	Thu	Fri	Weekly
Retention						
Conversion						
Leads						
Daily/Weekly Total						

Enter the total budgeted minutes and the total actual minutes in the template below. We recommend using two electronic calendars. One to budget and the other one for actual so it is easy to calculate the totals at the end of each day and week.

Week's Daily Consistency Rate And Week's Average						
Profitable Content	Mon	Tue	Wed	Thu	Fri	Weekly
Budget (B)						
Actual (A)						
Consistency Rate: A/B						

A weekly average consistency rate of less than 80% is a sign your association's profitable content creation and delivery is getting off track. If nothing is done to get back on track, it will be very difficult to achieve your leads, conversion and retention rate goals.

Q3. Week 2

What are the week's start and end dates? Enter your answers in the spaces provided.

Start Date: Monday ____________

End Date : Friday ______________

How many minutes have been budgeted in your electronic calendar for each profitable content category each day? Enter your answers in minutes in the template below.

Week's Budget In Minutes						
Profitable Content	**Mon**	**Tue**	**Wed**	**Thu**	**Fri**	**Week Total**
Retention						
Conversion						
Leads						
Daily/Weekly Total						

Enter the total budgeted minutes and the total actual minutes in the template below. We recommend using two electronic calendars. One to budget and the other one for actual so it is easy to calculate the totals at the end of each day and week.

Week's Daily Consistency Rate And Week's Average						
Profitable Content	**Mon**	**Tue**	**Wed**	**Thu**	**Fri**	**Week Average**
Budget (B)						
Actual (A)						
Consistency Rate: A/B						

A weekly average consistency rate of less than 80% is a sign your association's profitable content creation and delivery is getting off track. If nothing is done to get back on track, it will be difficult to achieve your leads, conversion and retention rate goals.

Q3. Week 3

What are the week's start and end dates? Enter your answers in the spaces provided.

Start Date: Monday ____________

End Date : Friday ______________

How many minutes have been budgeted in your electronic calendar for each profitable content category each day? Enter your answers in minutes in the template below.

Week's Budget In Minutes						
Profitable Content	**Mon**	**Tue**	**Wed**	**Thu**	**Fri**	**Week Total**
Retention						
Conversion						
Leads						
Daily/Weekly Total						

Enter the total budgeted minutes and the total actual minutes in the template below. We recommend using two electronic calendars. One to budget and the other one for actual so it is easy to calculate the totals at the end of each day and week.

Week's Daily Consistency Rate And Week's Average						
Profitable Content	**Mon**	**Tue**	**Wed**	**Thu**	**Fri**	**Week Average**
Budget (B)						
Actual (A)						
Consistency Rate: A/B						

A weekly average consistency rate of less than 80% is a sign your association's profitable content creation and delivery is getting off track. If nothing is done to get back on track, it will be very difficult to achieve your leads, conversion and retention rate goals.

Q3. Week 4

What are the week's start and end dates? Enter your answers in the spaces provided.

Start Date: Monday ______________

End Date : Friday ________________

How many minutes have been budgeted in your electronic calendar for each profitable content category each day? Enter your answers in minutes in the template below.

Week's Budget In Minutes						
Profitable Content	**Mon**	**Tue**	**Wed**	**Thu**	**Fri**	**Week Total**
Retention						
Conversion						
Leads						
Daily/Weekly Total						

Enter the total budgeted minutes and the total actual minutes in the template below. We recommend using two electronic calendars. One to budget and the other one for actual so it is easy to calculate the totals at the end of each day and week.

Week's Daily Consistency Rate And Week's Average						
Profitable Content	**Mon**	**Tue**	**Wed**	**Thu**	**Fri**	**Week Average**
Budget (B)						
Actual (A)						
Consistency Rate: A/B						

A weekly average consistency rate of less than 80% is a sign your association's profitable content creation and delivery is getting off track. If nothing is done to get back on track, it will be very difficult to achieve your leads, conversion and retention rate goals.

Q3. Week 5

What are the week's start and end dates? Enter your answers in the spaces provided.

Start Date: Monday ____________

End Date : Friday ______________

How many minutes have been budgeted in your electronic calendar for each profitable content category each day? Enter your answers in minutes in the template below.

Week's Budget In Minutes						
Profitable Content	**Mon**	**Tue**	**Wed**	**Thu**	**Fri**	**Week Total**
Retention						
Conversion						
Leads						
Daily/Weekly Total						

Enter the total budgeted minutes and the total actual minutes in the template below. We recommend using two electronic calendars. One to budget and the other one for actual so it is easy to calculate the totals at the end of each day and week.

Week's Daily Consistency Rate And Week's Average						
Profitable Content	**Mon**	**Tue**	**Wed**	**Thu**	**Fri**	**Week Average**
Budget (B)						
Actual (A)						
Consistency Rate: A/B						

A weekly average consistency rate of less than 80% is a sign your association's profitable content creation and delivery is getting off track. If nothing is done to get back on track, it will be very difficult to achieve your leads, conversion and retention rate goals.

Q3. Week 6

What are the week's start and end dates? Enter your answers in the spaces provided.

Start Date: Monday ____________

End Date : Friday ______________

How many minutes have been budgeted in your electronic calendar for each profitable content category each day? Enter your answers in minutes in the template below.

Week's Budget In Minutes						
Profitable Content	**Mon**	**Tue**	**Wed**	**Thu**	**Fri**	**Week Total**
Retention						
Conversion						
Leads						
Daily/Weekly Total						

Enter the total budgeted minutes and the total actual minutes in the template below. We recommend using two electronic calendars. One to budget and the other one for actual so it is easy to calculate the totals at the end of each day and week.

Week's Daily Consistency Rate And Week's Average						
Profitable Content	**Mon**	**Tue**	**Wed**	**Thu**	**Fri**	**Week Average**
Budget (B)						
Actual (A)						
Consistency Rate: A/B						

A weekly average consistency rate of less than 80% is a sign your association's profitable content creation and delivery is getting off track. If nothing is done to get back on track, it will be very difficult to achieve your leads, conversion and retention rate goals.

Q3. Week 7

What are the week's start and end dates? Enter your answers in the spaces provided.

Start Date: Monday ____________

End Date : Friday ________________

How many minutes have been budgeted in your electronic calendar for each profitable content category each day? Enter your answers in minutes in the template below.

Week's Budget In Minutes						
Profitable Content	**Mon**	**Tue**	**Wed**	**Thu**	**Fri**	**Week Total**
Retention						
Conversion						
Leads						
Daily/Weekly Total						

Enter the total budgeted minutes and the total actual minutes in the template below. We recommend using two electronic calendars. One to budget and the other one for actual so it is easy to calculate the totals at the end of each day and week.

Week's Daily Consistency Rate And Week's Average						
Profitable Content	**Mon**	**Tue**	**Wed**	**Thu**	**Fri**	**Week Average**
Budget (B)						
Actual (A)						
Consistency Rate: A/B						

A weekly average consistency rate of less than 80% is a sign your association's profitable content creation and delivery is getting off track. If nothing is done to get back on track, it will be very difficult to achieve your leads, conversion and retention rate goals.

Q3. Week 8

What are the week's start and end dates? Enter your answers in the spaces provided.

Start Date: Monday ____________

End Date : Friday ______________

How many minutes have been budgeted in your electronic calendar for each profitable content category each day? Enter your answers in minutes in the template below.

Week's Budget In Minutes						
Profitable Content	**Mon**	**Tue**	**Wed**	**Thu**	**Fri**	**Week Total**
Retention						
Conversion						
Leads						
Daily/Weekly Total						

Enter the total budgeted minutes and the total actual minutes in the template below. We recommend using two electronic calendars. One to budget and the other one for actual so it is easy to calculate the totals at the end of each day and week.

Week's Daily Consistency Rate And Week's Average						
Profitable Content	**Mon**	**Tue**	**Wed**	**Thu**	**Fri**	**Week Average**
Budget (B)						
Actual (A)						
Consistency Rate: A/B						

A weekly average consistency rate of less than 80% is a sign your association's profitable content creation and delivery is getting off track. If nothing is done to get back on track, it will be very difficult to achieve your leads, conversion and retention rate goals.

Q3. Week 9

What are the week's start and end dates? Enter your answers in the spaces provided.

Start Date: Monday _____________

End Date : Friday _______________

How many minutes have been budgeted in your electronic calendar for each profitable content category each day? Enter your answers in minutes in the template below.

Week's Budget In Minutes						
Profitable Content	**Mon**	**Tue**	**Wed**	**Thu**	**Fri**	**Week Total**
Retention						
Conversion						
Leads						
Daily/Weekly Total						

Enter the total budgeted minutes and the total actual minutes in the template below. We recommend using two electronic calendars. One to budget and the other one for actual so it is easy to calculate the totals at the end of each day and week.

Week's Daily Consistency Rate And Week's Average						
Profitable Content	**Mon**	**Tue**	**Wed**	**Thu**	**Fri**	**Week Average**
Budget (B)						
Actual (A)						
Consistency Rate: A/B						

A weekly average consistency rate of less than 80% is a sign your association's profitable content creation and delivery is getting off track. If nothing is done to get back on track, it will be very difficult to achieve your leads, conversion and retention rate goals.

Q3. Week 10

What are the week's start and end dates? Enter your answers in the spaces provided.

Start Date: Monday ____________

End Date : Friday ______________

How many minutes have been budgeted in your electronic calendar for each profitable content category each day? Enter your answers in minutes in the template below.

Week's Budget In Minutes						
Profitable Content	**Mon**	**Tue**	**Wed**	**Thu**	**Fri**	**Week Total**
Retention						
Conversion						
Leads						
Daily/Weekly Total						

Enter the total budgeted minutes and the total actual minutes in the template below. We recommend using two electronic calendars. One to budget and the other one for actual so it is easy to calculate the totals at the end of each day and week.

Week's Daily Consistency Rate And Week's Average						
Profitable Content	**Mon**	**Tue**	**Wed**	**Thu**	**Fri**	**Week Average**
Budget (B)						
Actual (A)						
Consistency Rate: A/B						

A weekly average consistency rate of less than 80% is a sign your association's profitable content creation and delivery is getting off track. If nothing is done to get back on track, it will be very difficult to achieve your leads, conversion and retention rate goals.

Q3. Week 11

What are the week's start and end dates? Enter your answers in the spaces provided.

Start Date: Monday ____________

End Date : Friday ______________

How many minutes have been budgeted in your electronic calendar for each profitable content category each day? Enter your answers in minutes in the template below.

Week's Budget In Minutes						
Profitable Content	**Mon**	**Tue**	**Wed**	**Thu**	**Fri**	**Week Total**
Retention						
Conversion						
Leads						
Daily/Weekly Total						

Enter the total budgeted minutes and the total actual minutes in the template below. We recommend using two electronic calendars. One to budget and the other one for actual so it is easy to calculate the totals at the end of each day and week.

Week's Daily Consistency Rate And Week's Average						
Profitable Content	**Mon**	**Tue**	**Wed**	**Thu**	**Fri**	**Week Average**
Budget (B)						
Actual (A)						
Consistency Rate: A/B						

A weekly average consistency rate of less than 80% is a sign your association's profitable content creation and delivery is getting off track. If nothing is done to get back on track, it will be very difficult to achieve your leads, conversion and retention rate goals.

Q3. Week 12

What are the week's start and end dates? Enter your answers in the spaces provided.

Start Date: Monday ____________

End Date : Friday ______________

How many minutes have been budgeted in your electronic calendar for each profitable content category each day? Enter your answers in minutes in the template below.

Week's Budget In Minutes						
Profitable Content	**Mon**	**Tue**	**Wed**	**Thu**	**Fri**	**Week Total**
Retention						
Conversion						
Leads						
Daily/Weekly Total						

Enter the total budgeted minutes and the total actual minutes in the template below. We recommend using two electronic calendars. One to budget and the other one for actual so it is easy to calculate the totals at the end of each day and week.

Week's Daily Consistency Rate And Week's Average						
Profitable Content	**Mon**	**Tue**	**Wed**	**Thu**	**Fri**	**Week Average**
Budget (B)						
Actual (A)						
Consistency Rate: A/B						

A weekly average consistency rate of less than 80% is a sign your association's profitable content creation and delivery is getting off track. If nothing is done to get back on track, it will be very difficult to achieve your leads, conversion and retention rate goals.

Q3. Week 13

What are the week's start and end dates? Enter your answers in the spaces provided.

Start Date: Monday ______________

End Date : Friday ________________

How many minutes have been budgeted in your electronic calendar for each profitable content category each day? Enter your answers in minutes in the template below.

Week's Budget In Minutes						
Profitable Content	**Mon**	**Tue**	**Wed**	**Thu**	**Fri**	**Week Total**
Retention						
Conversion						
Leads						

Enter the total budgeted minutes and the total actual minutes in the template below. We recommend using two electronic calendars. One to budget and the other one for actual so it is easy to calculate the totals at the end of each day and week.

Week's Daily Consistency Rate And Week's Average						
Profitable Content	**Mon**	**Tue**	**Wed**	**Thu**	**Fri**	**Week Average**
Budget (B)						
Actual (A)						
Consistency Rate: A/B						

A weekly average consistency rate of less than 80% is a sign your association's profitable content creation and delivery is getting off track. If nothing is done to get back on track, it will be very difficult to achieve your leads, conversion and retention rate goals.

Weekly Conversion Rate Scoreboard Example

Conversion Rate is simply a measure of the number of new members divided by the number of leads actually generated expressed as a percentage.

In major step 1 above, we were able to develop ABC's weekly map as follows:

ABC's New Members Map In Weeks					
Measures	**Q1**	**Q2**	**Q3**	**Q4**	**Total**
Leads Per Week	25	50	75	100	3250
Conversion Rate Per Week	20%	20%	20%	20%	20%
New Members Per Week	5	10	15	20	650

If ABC Association generates 20 leads and converts 15% of them in week 1 of Q1, the weekly accountability conversion rate scoreboard will look like this:

Q3: Week 1 Ending: 9/18/20 Weekly Conversion Rate Scoreboard				
Measures	QTD Budget	QTD Actual	Variance	Progress %
Leads	25	20	(5)	80%
Conversion Rate	20%	15%	(5)	75%
New Members	5	3	(2)	60%

Weekly Conversion Rate Scoreboard Interpretation Table	
Progress	
80% to 100%+ Progress	Green
60% to 79% Progress	Yellow
Less Than 60% Progress	Red

"Variance" is QTD Actual minus QTD Budget

These colors enable organizations to determine quickly how a measure is doing. Weekly scoreboard templates will be provided in the scoreboard templates section of this planner to enable your organization keep score weekly

Weekly Conversion Rate Scoreboard Templates

Enter your association's budget and actual numbers below and calculate the variance and progress %.

Q3: Week 1 Ending: ___________Weekly Conversion Rate Scoreboard				
Measures	QTD Budget	QTD Actual	Variance	Progress %
Leads				
Conversion Rate				
New Members				
Q3: Week 2 Ending: ___________ Weekly Conversion Rate Scoreboard				
Measures	QTD Budget	QTD Actual	Variance	Progress %
Leads				
Conversion Rate				
New Members				

Q3: Week 3 Ending: ___________ Weekly Conversion Rate Scoreboard				
Measures	QTD Budget	QTD Actual	Variance	Progress %
Leads				
Conversion Rate				
New Members				

Q3: Week 4 Ending: ___________ Weekly Conversion Rate Scoreboard				
Measures	QTD Budget	QTD Actual	Variance	Progress %
Leads				
Conversion Rate				
New Members				

Q3: Week 5 Ending: ___________ Weekly Conversion Rate Scoreboard				
Measures	QTD Budget	QTD Actual	Variance	Progress %
Leads				
Conversion Rate				
New Members				

Q3: Week 6 Ending: ___________ Weekly Conversion Rate Scoreboard				
Measures	QTD Budget	QTD Actual	Variance	Progress %
Leads				
Conversion Rate				
New Members				

Q3: Week 7 Ending: ___________ Weekly Conversion Rate Scoreboard				
Measures	QTD Budget	QTD Actual	Variance	Progress %
Leads				
Conversion Rate				
New Members				

Q3: Week 8 Ending: ___________ Weekly Conversion Rate Scoreboard				
Measures	QTD Budget	QTD Actual	Variance	Progress %
Leads				
Conversion Rate				
New Members				

Q3: Week 9 Ending: ___________ Weekly Conversion Rate Scoreboard				
Measures	QTD Budget	QTD Actual	Variance	Progress %
Leads				
Conversion Rate				
New Members				

Q3: Week 10 Ending: ___________ Weekly Conversion Rate Scoreboard				
Measures	QTD Budget	QTD Actual	Variance	Progress %
Leads				
Conversion Rate				
New Members				

Q3: Week 11 Ending: ___________ Weekly Conversion Rate Scoreboard				
Measures	QTD Budget	QTD Actual	Variance	Progress %
Leads				
Conversion Rate				
New Members				

Q3: Week 12 Ending: ___________ Weekly Conversion Rate Scoreboard				
Measures	QTD Budget	QTD Actual	Variance	Progress %
Leads				
Conversion Rate				
New Members				

Q3: Week 13 Ending: ___________Weekly Conversion Rate Scoreboard				
Measures	QTD Budget	QTD Actual	Variance	Progress %
Leads				
Conversion Rate				
New Members				

Quarterly Retention Rate Example

Quarterly retention rates will enable your organization to determine how your retention content is performing.

To calculate your organization's retention rate at the end of each quarter, take the following steps:

Step 1: Identify the number of members at the beginning of the quarter

Step 2: Identify the number of new members who were added during the quarter

Step 3: Identify the number of members at the end of the quarter

Step 4: Calculate the retention number by subtracting new members number from end of quarter number.

Step 5: Calculate the retention rate by dividing the retention number calculated in step 4 by the beginning number.

ABC Association Example:

Here are the five steps using ABC Association's projected membership numbers:

Step 1: Q3 Beginning number: 4500

Step 2: Q3 New members addition 60

Step 3: Q3 Ending number: 4000

Step 4: Q3 Retention number: 4000 – 60 = 3940

Step 5: Q3 Retention rate: 3940/4500 = 88%

Based on ABC Association's budgeted retention rate of 90%, the retention rate scoreboard will look as follows:

Q3: Ending: 12/31/20 Quarterly Retention Rate Scoreboard				
Measure	QTD Budget	QTD Actual	Variance	Progress %
Retention Rate	90%	88%	(2)	98%

Quarterly Retention Rate Scoreboard Interpretation Table	
Progress	
90% to 100%+ Progress	Green
70% to 89% Progress	Yellow
Less Than 70% Progress	Red

"Variance" is QTD Actual minus QTD Budget

These colors enable organizations to determine quickly how their retention rate is progressing. Quarterly scoreboard templates will be provided in the scoreboard templates section of this planner to enable your organization keep score quarterly.

Quarterly Retention Rate Scoreboard Template

Enter the quarter's ending date and follow the five steps above to calculate your association's retention rate for the quarter and compare it to the budgeted retention rate established in major step 1 above.

Q3: Ending: Quarterly Retention Rate Scoreboard				
Measure	QTD Budget	QTD Actual	Variance	Progress %
Retention Rate				

Daily Consistency Rate Scoreboard Templates

Q4. Week 1

What are the week's start and end dates? Enter your answers in the spaces provided.

Start Date: Monday ____________

End Date : Friday ______________

How many minutes have been budgeted in your electronic calendar for each profitable content category each day? Enter your answers in minutes in the template below.

Week's Budget In Minutes						
Profitable Content	**Mon**	**Tue**	**Wed**	**Thu**	**Fri**	**Weekly**
Retention						
Conversion						
Leads						
Daily/Weekly Total						

Enter the total budgeted minutes and the total actual minutes in the template below. We recommend using two electronic calendars. One to budget and the other one for actual so it is easy to calculate the totals at the end of each day and week.

Week's Daily Consistency Rate And Week's Average						
Profitable Content	**Mon**	**Tue**	**Wed**	**Thu**	**Fri**	**Weekly**
Budget (B)						
Actual (A)						
Consistency Rate: A/B						

A weekly average consistency rate of less than 80% is a sign your association's profitable content creation and delivery is getting off track. If nothing is done to get back on track, it will be very difficult to achieve your leads, conversion and retention rate goals.

Q4. Week 2

What are the week's start and end dates? Enter your answers in the spaces provided.

How many minutes have been budgeted in your electronic calendar for each profitable content category each day? Enter your answers in minutes in the template below.

Start Date: Monday ____________

End Date : Friday ______________

Week's Budget In Minutes						
Profitable Content	**Mon**	**Tue**	**Wed**	**Thu**	**Fri**	**Week Total**
Retention						
Conversion						
Leads						
Daily/Weekly Total						

Enter the total budgeted minutes and the total actual minutes in the template below. We recommend using two electronic calendars. One to budget and the other one for actual so it is easy to calculate the totals at the end of each day and week.

Week's Daily Consistency Rate And Week's Average						
Profitable Content	**Mon**	**Tue**	**Wed**	**Thu**	**Fri**	**Week Average**
Budget (B)						
Actual (A)						
Consistency Rate: A/B						

A weekly average consistency rate of less than 80% is a sign your association's profitable content creation and delivery is getting off track. If nothing is done to get back on track, it will be difficult to achieve your leads, conversion and retention rate goals.

Q4. Week 3

What are the week's start and end dates? Enter your answers in the spaces provided.

Start Date: Monday ____________

End Date : Friday ______________

How many minutes have been budgeted in your electronic calendar for each profitable content category each day? Enter your answers in minutes in the template below.

Week's Budget In Minutes						
Profitable Content	Mon	Tue	Wed	Thu	Fri	Week Total
Retention						
Conversion						
Leads						
Daily/Weekly Total						

Enter the total budgeted minutes and the total actual minutes in the template below. We recommend using two electronic calendars. One to budget and the other one for actual so it is easy to calculate the totals at the end of each day and week.

Week's Daily Consistency Rate And Week's Average						
Profitable Content	Mon	Tue	Wed	Thu	Fri	Week Average
Budget (B)						
Actual (A)						
Consistency Rate: A/B						

A weekly average consistency rate of less than 80% is a sign your association's profitable content creation and delivery is getting off track. If nothing is done to get back on track, it will be very difficult to achieve your leads, conversion and retention rate goals.

Q4. Week 4

What are the week's start and end dates? Enter your answers in the spaces provided.

Start Date: Monday ____________

End Date : Friday ______________

How many minutes have been budgeted in your electronic calendar for each profitable content category each day? Enter your answers in minutes in the template below.

Week's Budget In Minutes						
Profitable Content	Mon	Tue	Wed	Thu	Fri	Week Total
Retention						
Conversion						
Leads						
Daily/Weekly Total						

Enter the total budgeted minutes and the total actual minutes in the template below. We recommend using two electronic calendars. One to budget and the other one for actual so it is easy to calculate the totals at the end of each day and week.

Week's Daily Consistency Rate And Week's Average						
Profitable Content	**Mon**	**Tue**	**Wed**	**Thu**	**Fri**	**Week Average**
Budget (B)						
Actual (A)						
Consistency Rate: A/B						

A weekly average consistency rate of less than 80% is a sign your association's profitable content creation and delivery is getting off track. If nothing is done to get back on track, it will be very difficult to achieve your leads, conversion and retention rate goals.

Q4. Week 5

What are the week's start and end dates? Enter your answers in the spaces provided.

Start Date: Monday ____________

End Date : Friday ______________

How many minutes have been budgeted in your electronic calendar for each profitable content category each day? Enter your answers in minutes in the template below

Week's Budget In Minutes						
Profitable Content	**Mon**	**Tue**	**Wed**	**Thu**	**Fri**	**Week Total**
Retention						
Conversion						
Leads						
Daily/Weekly Total						

Enter the total budgeted minutes and the total actual minutes in the template below. We recommend using two electronic calendars. One to budget and the other one for actual so it is easy to calculate the totals at the end of each day and week.

Week's Daily Consistency Rate And Week's Average						
Profitable Content	**Mon**	**Tue**	**Wed**	**Thu**	**Fri**	**Week Average**
Budget (B)						
Actual (A)						
Consistency Rate: A/B						

A weekly average consistency rate of less than 80% is a sign your association's profitable content creation and delivery is getting off track. If nothing is done to get back on track, it will be very difficult to achieve your leads, conversion and retention rate goals.

Q4. Week 6

What are the week's start and end dates? Enter your answers in the spaces provided.

Start Date: Monday ____________

End Date : Friday ______________

How many minutes have been budgeted in your electronic calendar for each profitable content category each day? Enter your answers in minutes in the template below.

Week's Budget In Minutes						
Profitable Content	**Mon**	**Tue**	**Wed**	**Thu**	**Fri**	**Week Total**
Retention						
Conversion						
Leads						
Daily/Weekly Total						

Enter the total budgeted minutes and the total actual minutes in the template below. We recommend using two electronic calendars. One to budget and the other one for actual so it is easy to calculate the totals at the end of each day and week.

Week's Daily Consistency Rate And Week's Average						
Profitable Content	**Mon**	**Tue**	**Wed**	**Thu**	**Fri**	**Week Average**
Budget (B)						
Actual (A)						
Consistency Rate: A/B						

A weekly average consistency rate of less than 80% is a sign your association's profitable content creation and delivery is getting off track. If nothing is done to get back on track, it will be very difficult to achieve your leads, conversion and retention rate goals.

Q4. Week 7

What are the week's start and end dates? Enter your answers in the spaces provided.

Start Date: Monday ______________

End Date : Friday ________________

How many minutes have been budgeted in your electronic calendar for each profitable content category each day? Enter your answers in minutes in the template below.

Week's Budget In Minutes						
Profitable Content	**Mon**	**Tue**	**Wed**	**Thu**	**Fri**	**Week Total**
Retention						
Conversion						
Leads						
Daily/Weekly Total						

Enter the total budgeted minutes and the total actual minutes in the template below. We recommend using two electronic calendars. One to budget and the other one for actual so it is easy to calculate the totals at the end of each day and week.

Week's Daily Consistency Rate And Week's Average						
Profitable Content	**Mon**	**Tue**	**Wed**	**Thu**	**Fri**	**Week Average**
Budget (B)						
Actual (A)						
Consistency Rate: A/B						

A weekly average consistency rate of less than 80% is a sign your association's profitable content creation and delivery is getting off track. If nothing is done to get back on track, it will be very difficult to achieve your leads, conversion and retention rate goals.

Q4. Week 8

What are the week's start and end dates? Enter your answers in the spaces provided.

Start Date: Monday ______________

End Date : Friday ________________

How many minutes have been budgeted in your electronic calendar for each profitable content category each day? Enter your answers in minutes in the template below.

Week's Budget In Minutes						
Profitable Content	**Mon**	**Tue**	**Wed**	**Thu**	**Fri**	**Week Total**
Retention						
Conversion						
Leads						
Daily/Weekly Total						

Enter the total budgeted minutes and the total actual minutes in the template below. We recommend using two electronic calendars. One to budget and the other one for actual so it is easy to calculate the totals at the end of each day and week.

Week's Daily Consistency Rate And Week's Average						
Profitable Content	**Mon**	**Tue**	**Wed**	**Thu**	**Fri**	**Week Average**
Budget (B)						
Actual (A)						
Consistency Rate: A/B						

A weekly average consistency rate of less than 80% is a sign your association's profitable content creation and delivery is getting off track. If nothing is done to get back on track, it will be very difficult to achieve your leads, conversion and retention rate goals.

Q4. Week 9

What are the week's start and end dates? Enter your answers in the spaces provided.

Start Date: Monday ____________

End Date : Friday ______________

How many minutes have been budgeted in your electronic calendar for each profitable content category each day? Enter your answers in minutes in the template below.

Week's Budget In Minutes						
Profitable Content	**Mon**	**Tue**	**Wed**	**Thu**	**Fri**	**Week Total**
Retention						
Conversion						
Leads						
Daily/Weekly Total						

Enter the total budgeted minutes and the total actual minutes in the template below. We recommend using two electronic calendars. One to budget and the other one for actual so it is easy to calculate the totals at the end of each day and week.

Week's Daily Consistency Rate And Week's Average						
Profitable Content	**Mon**	**Tue**	**Wed**	**Thu**	**Fri**	**Week Average**
Budget (B)						
Actual (A)						
Consistency Rate: A/B						

A weekly average consistency rate of less than 80% is a sign your association's profitable content creation and delivery is getting off track. If nothing is done to get back on track, it will be very difficult to achieve your leads, conversion and retention rate goals.

Q4. Week 10

What are the week's start and end dates? Enter your answers in the spaces provided.

Start Date: Monday ______________

End Date : Friday ________________

How many minutes have been budgeted in your electronic calendar for each profitable content category each day? Enter your answers in minutes in the template below.

Week's Budget In Minutes						
Profitable Content	**Mon**	**Tue**	**Wed**	**Thu**	**Fri**	**Week Total**
Retention						
Conversion						
Leads						
Daily/Weekly Total						

Enter the total budgeted minutes and the total actual minutes in the template below. We recommend using two electronic calendars. One to budget and the other one for actual so it is easy to calculate the totals at the end of each day and week.

Week's Daily Consistency Rate And Week's Average						
Profitable Content	**Mon**	**Tue**	**Wed**	**Thu**	**Fri**	**Week Average**
Budget (B)						
Actual (A)						
Consistency Rate: A/B						

A weekly average consistency rate of less than 80% is a sign your association's profitable content creation and delivery is getting off track. If nothing is done to get back on track, it will be very difficult to achieve your leads, conversion and retention rate goals.

Q4. Week 11

What are the week's start and end dates? Enter your answers in the spaces provided.

Start Date: Monday ____________

End Date : Friday ______________

How many minutes have been budgeted in your electronic calendar for each profitable content category each day? Enter your answers in minutes in the template below.

Week's Budget In Minutes						
Profitable Content	**Mon**	**Tue**	**Wed**	**Thu**	**Fri**	**Week Total**
Retention						
Conversion						
Leads						
Daily/Weekly Total						

Enter the total budgeted minutes and the total actual minutes in the template below. We recommend using two electronic calendars. One to budget and the other one for actual so it is easy to calculate the totals at the end of each day and week.

Week's Daily Consistency Rate And Week's Average						
Profitable Content	**Mon**	**Tue**	**Wed**	**Thu**	**Fri**	**Week Average**
Budget (B)						
Actual (A)						
Consistency Rate: A/B						

A weekly average consistency rate of less than 80% is a sign your association's profitable content creation and delivery is getting off track. If nothing is done to get back on track, it will be very difficult to achieve your leads, conversion and retention rate goals.

Q4. Week 12

What are the week's start and end dates? Enter your answers in the spaces provided.

Start Date: Monday ______________

End Date : Friday _______________

How many minutes have been budgeted in your electronic calendar for each profitable content category each day? Enter your answers in minutes in the template below.

Week's Budget In Minutes						
Profitable Content	**Mon**	**Tue**	**Wed**	**Thu**	**Fri**	**Week Total**
Retention						
Conversion						
Leads						
Daily/Weekly Total						

Enter the total budgeted minutes and the total actual minutes in the template below. We recommend using two electronic calendars. One to budget and the other one for actual so it is easy to calculate the totals at the end of each day and week.

Week's Daily Consistency Rate And Week's Average						
Profitable Content	**Mon**	**Tue**	**Wed**	**Thu**	**Fri**	**Week Average**
Budget (B)						
Actual (A)						
Consistency Rate: A/B						

A weekly average consistency rate of less than 80% is a sign your association's profitable content creation and delivery is getting off track. If nothing is done to get back on track, it will be very difficult to achieve your leads, conversion and retention rate goals.

Q4. Week 13

What are the week's start and end dates? Enter your answers in the spaces provided.

Start Date: Monday ____________

End Date : Friday ______________

How many minutes have been budgeted in your electronic calendar for each profitable content category each day? Enter your answers in minutes in the template below.

Week's Budget In Minutes						
Profitable Content	**Mon**	**Tue**	**Wed**	**Thu**	**Fri**	**Week Total**
Retention						
Conversion						
Leads						
Daily/Weekly Total						

Enter the total budgeted minutes and the total actual minutes in the template below. We recommend using two electronic calendars. One to budget and the other one for actual so it is easy to calculate the totals at the end of each day and week.

Week's Daily Consistency Rate And Week's Average						
Profitable Content	**Mon**	**Tue**	**Wed**	**Thu**	**Fri**	**Week Average**
Budget (B)						
Actual (A)						
Consistency Rate: A/B						

A weekly average consistency rate of less than 80% is a sign your association's profitable content creation and delivery is getting off track. If nothing is done to get back on track, it will be very difficult to achieve your leads, conversion and retention rate goals.

Weekly Conversion Rate Scoreboard Example

Conversion Rate is simply a measure of the number of new members divided by the number of leads actually generated expressed as a percentage.

In major step 1 above, we were able to develop ABC's weekly map as follows:

ABC's New Members Map In Weeks					
Measures	**Q1**	**Q2**	**Q3**	**Q4**	**Total**
Leads Per Week	25	50	75	100	3250
Conversion Rate Per Week	20%	20%	20%	20%	20%
New Members Per Week	5	10	15	20	650

If ABC Association generates 20 leads and converts 15% of them in week 1 of Q1, the weekly accountability conversion rate scoreboard will look like this:

Q4: Week 1 Ending: _______ Weekly Conversion Rate Scoreboard				
Measures	QTD Budget	QTD Actual	Variance	Progress %
Leads	25	20	(5)	80%
Conversion Rate	20%	15%	(5)	75%
New Members	5	3	(2)	60%

Weekly Conversion Rate Scoreboard Interpretation Table	
Progress	
80% to 100%+ Progress	Green
60% to 79% Progress	Yellow
Less Than 60% Progress	Red

"Variance" is QTD Actual minus QTD Budget

These colors enable organizations to determine quickly how a measure is doing. Weekly scoreboard templates will be provided in the scoreboard templates section of this planner to enable your organization keep score weekly

Weekly Conversion Rate Scoreboard Templates

Enter your association's budget and actual numbers below and calculate the variance and progress %.

Q4: Week 1 Ending: __________ Weekly Conversion Rate Scoreboard				
Measures	QTD Budget	QTD Actual	Variance	Progress %
Leads				
Conversion Rate				
New Members				
Q4: Week 2 Ending: __________ Weekly Conversion Rate Scoreboard				
Measures	QTD Budget	QTD Actual	Variance	Progress %
Leads				
Conversion Rate				
New Members				

Q4: Week 3 Ending: ____________Weekly Conversion Rate Scoreboard				
Measures	QTD Budget	QTD Actual	Variance	Progress %
Leads				
Conversion Rate				
New Members				

Q4: Week 4 Ending:____________Weekly Conversion Rate Scoreboard				
Measures	QTD Budget	QTD Actual	Variance	Progress %
Leads				
Conversion Rate				
New Members				

Q4: Week 5 Ending:____________Weekly Conversion Rate Scoreboard				
Measures	QTD Budget	QTD Actual	Variance	Progress %
Leads				
Conversion Rate				
New Members				

Q4: Week 6 Ending: ____________ Weekly Conversion Rate Scoreboard				
Measures	QTD Budget	QTD Actual	Variance	Progress %
Leads				
Conversion Rate				
New Members				

Q4: Week 7 Ending: ____________Weekly Conversion Rate Scoreboard				
Measures	QTD Budget	QTD Actual	Variance	Progress %
Leads				
Conversion Rate				
New Members				

Q4: Week 8 Ending: ___________Weekly Conversion Rate Scoreboard				
Measures	QTD Budget	QTD Actual	Variance	Progress %
Leads				
Conversion Rate				
New Members				

Q4: Week 9 Ending: ___________ Weekly Conversion Rate Scoreboard				
Measures	QTD Budget	QTD Actual	Variance	Progress %
Leads				
Conversion Rate				
New Members				

Q4: Week 10 Ending: ___________ Weekly Conversion Rate Scoreboard				
Measures	QTD Budget	QTD Actual	Variance	Progress %
Leads				
Conversion Rate				
New Members				

Q4: Week 11 Ending: ___________ Weekly Conversion Rate Scoreboard				
Measures	QTD Budget	QTD Actual	Variance	Progress %
Leads				
Conversion Rate				
New Members				

Q4: Week 12 Ending: ___________ Weekly Conversion Rate Scoreboard				
Measures	QTD Budget	QTD Actual	Variance	Progress %
Leads				
Conversion Rate				
New Members				

Q4: Week 13 Ending: ___________ Weekly Conversion Rate Scoreboard				
Measures	QTD Budget	QTD Actual	Variance	Progress %
Leads				
Conversion Rate				
New Members				

Quarterly Retention Rate Example

Quarterly retention rates will enable your organization to determine how your retention content is performing.

To calculate your organization's retention rate at the end of each quarter, take the following steps:

Step 1: Identify the number of members at the beginning of the quarter

Step 2: Identify the number of new members who were added during the quarter

Step 3: Identify the number of members at the end of the quarter

Step 4: Calculate the retention number by subtracting new members number from end of quarter number.

Step 5: Calculate the retention rate by dividing the retention number calculated in step 4 by the beginning number.

ABC Association Example:

Here are the five steps using ABC Association's projected membership numbers:

Step 1: Q4 Beginning number: 4500

Step 2: Q4 New members addition 60

Step 3: Q4 Ending number: 4000

Step 4: Q4 Retention number: 4000 – 60 = 3940

Step 5: Q4 Retention rate: 3940/4500 = 88%

Based on ABC Association's budgeted retention rate of 90%, the retention rate scoreboard will look as follows:

Q4: Ending: 12/31/20 Quarterly Retention Rate Scoreboard				
Measure	QTD Budget	QTD Actual	Variance	Progress %
Retention Rate	90%	88%	(2)	98%

Quarterly Retention Rate Scorecard Interpretation Table	
Progress	
90% to 100%+ Progress	Green
70% to 89% Progress	Yellow
Less Than 70% Progress	Red

"Variance" is QTD Actual minus QTD Budget

These colors enable organizations to determine quickly how their retention rate is progressing. Quarterly scoreboard templates will be provided in the scoreboard templates section of this planner to enable your organization keep score quarterly.

Quarterly Retention Rate Scoreboard Template

Enter the quarter's ending date and follow the five steps above to calculate your association's retention rate for the quarter and compare it to the budgeted retention rate established in major step 1 above.

Year Ending: Quarterly Retention Rate Scoreboard				
Measure	QTD Budget	QTD Actual	Variance	Progress %
Retention Rate				

Notes

Yearly Membership Scoreboard

To establish a yearly membership scoreboard, take the following steps:

Step 1: Total Leads

Enter the total number of leads budgeted for the year under YTD Budget column. Add up the total number of leads actually generated in Q1,Q2, Q3 and Q4 and enter the number under the YTD Actual column. Calculate the variance and the progress %.

Step 2: Average Conversion Rate

Enter the budgeted conversion rate under YTD Budget column. Calculate the average conversion for Q1,Q2, Q3 and Q4 and enter the number under the YTD Actual column. Calculate the variance and the progress %.

Step 3: Total Membership

Enter the budgeted number of members under the YTD Budget column. Add up the total number of members who joined in Q1,Q2, Q3 and Q4 and enter the number under the YTD Actual column. Calculate the variance and the progress %.

Step 4: Average Retention Rate

Enter the budgeted retention rate under YTD Budget column. Calculate the average retention rate for Q1, Q2, Q3 and Q4 and enter the number under the YTD Actual column. Calculate the variance and the progress %.

Year Ending: ________ Yearly Membership Scoreboard				
Measure	**YTD Budget**	**YTD Actual**	**Variance**	**Progress %**
Leads				
Conversion Rate				
Members				
Retention Rate				

This yearly scoreboard captures the annual results of an association and provides a benchmark for the following year's plan or map.

Notes

About the Author

Leona P. Dalavai Scott understands the everyday challenges that come with creating helpful and relevant content. She has more than 20 years of experience in the magazine publishing, print and digital environments working for professional business and trade associations. She draws on her personal experience, combined with in-depth research and case studies, to show how associations can thrive in today's environment to structure their content that builds value, grows membership and boosts retention.

In 2018, she began Profitable Content Menu to help organizations create relevant and helpful content to generate leads and convert those leads into members/customers for lifetime value. She wants to help associations use the three different types of content – retention, conversion and lead generation – to accomplish their membership goals. You can find her blogging about these topics at **ProfitableContentMenu.com**.

A graduate of the University of Kansas, she has a B.S. in journalism and a B.A. in political science. She lives in North Texas with her family, serving as a marketing communications consultant.

PROFITABLE
CONTENT
MENU

Book a free one-hour content strategy session with Leona by visiting her website at ***ProfitableContentMenu.com.*** *Learn how you can apply the C.O.N.T.E.N.T. Solution to grow your organization's membership.*